Books by the Same Author

BP738   Google for the Older Generation
BP735   Windows 8 Explained
BP284   Programming in QuickBASIC
BP259   A Concise Introduction to UNIX
BP258   Learning to Program in C
BP250   Programming in Fortran 77

Books Written with Phil Oliver

BP726   Microsoft Excel 2010 Explained
BP719   Microsoft Office 2010 Explained
BP718   Windows 7 Explained
BP710   An Introduction to Windows Live Essentials
BP706   An Introduction to Windows 7
BP703   An Introduction to Windows Vista
BP595   Google Explored
BP590   Microsoft Access 2007 explained
BP585   Microsoft Excel 2007 explained
BP584   Microsoft Word 2007 explained
BP583   Microsoft Office 2007 explained
BP581   Windows Vista explained
BP580   Windows Vista for Beginners
BP569   Microsoft Works 8.0 & Works Suite 2006 explained
BP563   Using Windows XP's Accessories
BP557   How Did I Do That ... in Windows XP
BP555   Using PDF Files
BP550   Advanced Guide to Windows XP
BP545   Paint Shop Pro 8 explained
BP538   Windows XP for Beginners
BP525   Controlling Windows XP the easy way
BP514   Windows XP explained
BP509   Microsoft Office XP explained
BP498   Using Visual Basic
BP341   MS-DOS explained

Windows 8
Explained

by

N. Kantaris

Bernard Babani (publishing) Ltd
The Grampians
Shepherds Bush Road
London W6 7NF
England

www.babanibooks.com

Please Note

Although every care has been taken with the production of this book to ensure that all information is correct at the time of writing and that any projects, designs, modifications and/or programs, etc., contained herewith, operate in a correct and safe manner and also that any components specified are normally available in Great Britain, the Publishers and Author(s) do not accept responsibility in any way for the failure (including fault in design) of any project, design, modification or program to work correctly or to cause damage to any equipment that it may be connected to or used in conjunction with, or in respect of any other damage or injury that may be so caused, nor do the Publishers accept responsibility in any way for the failure to obtain specified components.

Notice is also given that if equipment that is still under warranty is modified in any way or used or connected with home-built equipment then that warranty may be void.

First Published - February 2013

British Library Cataloguing in Publication Data:

A catalogue record for this book is available from the British Library

ISBN 978 0 85934 735 8

Cover Design by Gregor Arthur

Printed and bound in Great Britain for Bernard Babani (publishing) Ltd

Historical Background

In 1983, Microsoft launched the first version of Windows which was in reality a graphical extension to its Disc Operating System (MS-DOS).

In November 1985, Microsoft shipped Windows 1.0 which allowed you to use a mouse to point and click instead of having to type MS-DOS commands. This was followed in December 1987 with the release of Windows 2.0 which was designed for the Intel 286 processor. Windows/386 soon followed to take advantage of the advent of Intel 386 processor.

In May 1990, Microsoft produced an Intel 386 processor specific version of Windows which was able to run in multiple 'virtual 8086' mode, but Windows applications were unable to use any extended memory above 1 MB. In 1990, however, **Windows version 3.0** solved this problem and became a huge success.

In 1992, Microsoft released the much needed updated version **Windows 3.1** which fixed most of the program bugs in the previous version. **Windows for Workgroups 3.1**, followed in October 1992, and started to give the program the power to control small networked groups of computers. This was strengthened in October 1993 with the **Windows 3.11** release, which included 32-bit file management and more networking support.

In August 1995, Microsoft released **Windows 95**, a 32-bit operating system in its own right which made full use of the 32-bit features of the then available range of Intel processor chips. Microsoft had also put a lot of effort into this system to make it compatible with almost all existing Windows and MS-DOS based applications. This meant that parts of this version of Windows were still only 16-bit in operation.

In June 1998, Microsoft launched **Windows 98** which ran faster, crashed less frequently and supported a host of new technologies.

Windows 98 improvements included the ability to find information more easily on a PC as well as the Internet, open and close programs faster and supported DVDs for storing digital video, and improved MMX multimedia. In May 1999, **Windows 98 Second Edition** was released. **Windows 98** also introduced the 'Quick Launch' bar which allowed programs to run without having to browse the Start, All Programs menu or look for their desktop shortcut icon. **Windows 98** was the last version of Windows based on MS-DOS.

In September 2000, Microsoft released **Windows Me**, as the direct upgrade to Windows 95/98 for the home PC. **Windows Me** loaded faster and ran more reliably. In addition, it incorporated Wizards that let you set up home networks and share Internet connections, had improved support for digital cameras, video recorders, and multimedia with the introduction of the Windows Media Player 7.

In February 2000, Microsoft released **Windows 2000 Professional**, together with two additional **Windows NT** compatible versions of the software; Server and Advanced Server. Users of Windows 95/98 could easily upgrade to the **Windows 2000 Professional** version of this Operating System (OS), while users of **Windows NT** could upgrade to one of the other two versions of the OS.

In October 2001, Microsoft released **Windows XP** (XP for eXPerience) in two flavours; the Home edition (less expensive) as the direct upgrade to Windows 98/Me for home users and the Professional edition (more expensive but with additional functionality) for Windows 2000 or business users. **Windows XP** looked different to previous versions of Windows – there were changes to the desktop icons, start menu and the Control Panel, while other concepts were borrowed from Windows Me or Windows 2000.

There followed two major updates in the form of **Service Pack 1** (**SP1**) and, in August 2004, **Service Pack 2** (**SP2**). The latter update focused mainly on security of the computer, and was over 260 MB in size. Microsoft made security the central theme of SP2, although there were some additional features that were not specifically geared to security.

In late 2006, Microsoft launched **Windows Vista** with software that allowed you to browse the Web, send and receive e-mail messages, burn CDs and DVDs, edit photos and videos, and improved home entertainment. It also came with a range of security tools. BUT the hardware industry was slow to produce drivers for Vista and it developed a reputation for not working well with peripheral equipment.

In October 2009, **Windows 7** was finally released after many months of successful testing by millions of end users. The result is the best operating system so far produced, arguably by anyone.

Finally, in October 2012 **Windows 8** was released with its Modern interface – the subject of this book. **Windows 8** reflects the users preference for portable computing and constant connectivity via the Cloud. The Modern interface presents a radical redesign of the operating system and looks similar to the Windows Phone interface. It allows live information to be displayed on its tiles and supports both traditional keyboard and touch-screen devices. **Windows 8** comes pre-loaded with a number of Apps, such as Mail, Internet Explorer, People, Calendar, Maps, Photos, Music, Video and Messaging, with additional Apps available from the Windows Apps Store. This is a truly different operating system from previous versions of Windows, but worth the extra learning curve.

About this Book

Windows 8 Explained was written so that you can quickly explore the workings of Microsoft's new Windows operating system. Windows 8 is not the result of evolution from previous versions of Windows, but a brand new product designed to interface seamlessly with your Desktop, Laptop or X86 Tablet. Windows 8 manages the available resources of your computer and 'controls' the programs that run on it. To get the most from your various devices, it is important that you have a good working knowledge of its Operating System (OS) which in this case is Windows 8.

The book covers the Windows 8 environment with its new Modern interface (as shown above), many Apps and general controls. Chapters include:

- An overview of the stylish new interface, including the Modern interface, Desktop, Taskbar, running Apps, the Tray Notification Area and using the Charms bar.

- How to manage Windows Settings, User Accounts, Personalise your PC, control your System and work with programs.

- How to use the Desktop File Explorer and the Internet Explorer and how to use the e-mail App to keep in touch with friends and family.

- How to use SkyDrive and use shared folders.

- How to work with and organise your digital photographs and import them from your camera.

- Using bing maps to search for locations, services and get driving directions, as well as help with public transport.

- Manage the News, Finance and Weather Apps.

- Use the Windows Media Player to store and play your music, burn CDs and install Media Center to access the DVD playback facility.

- Connect to wireless networks and set up a HomeGroup, share a printer and network PCs running Windows 8 and Windows 7. How to use mobility tools to keep your laptop running while away from home.

- How to generally control your PC, keep it healthy, backup your important files and how to use Accessibility features if you have problems using the keyboard or mouse or have poor eyesight.

- How to use the new Paint and WordPad Apps.

The material in the book is presented using everyday language, avoiding jargon as much as possible. It was written with the non technical, non computer literate person in mind.

This book applies to; **Windows 8**, **8 Pro** and the vast majority of **Windows 8 Enterprise**. Also, parts of the book should be applicable to **Windows RT** which is built on the same foundation as Windows 8, but is a restricted version designed specifically for ARM Tablets.

I hope that with the help of this book, you will be able to get the most out of your computer when using Windows 8, and that you will be able to do it in the shortest, most effective and enjoyable way. Most of all, have fun!

About the Author

Noel Kantaris graduated in Electrical Engineering at Bristol University and after spending three years in the Electronics Industry in London, took up a Tutorship in Physics at the University of Queensland. Research interests in Ionospheric Physics, led to the degrees of M.E. in Electronics and Ph.D. in Physics. On return to the UK, he took up a Post-Doctoral Research Fellowship in Radio Physics at the University of Leicester, and then a lecturing position in Engineering at the Camborne School of Mines, Cornwall, (part of Exeter University), where he was also the CSM Computing Manager. Lately he also served as IT Director of FFC Ltd.

Trademarks

Contents

1

Windows 8 Overview

Microsoft have really produced a stunning operating system with Windows 8. What you see above is the Modern interface with live tiles. These will launch an application, but also have the ability to display live information such as new e-mail messages. The tiles are grouped in three sets: in the left set there are Apps to access (from left to right) **Mail**, **Internet Explorer**, **Store**, **Calendar, Maps**, **SkyDrive**, etc. In the middle set, Apps access **Bing** (the Internet search engine), **Travel**, **Finance**, etc., while on the right set you'll find the programs you have installed. Tapping or left-clicking any of these tiles, starts the appropriate App or program.

Windows 8 not only looks good, but it performs very well indeed, it is fast to load and is stylish. At first you might be puzzled not knowing how to configure your computer or change screens, but don't worry, all will be explained in good time! This is a brand new product with a brand new interface.

Windows 8 is the most secure version of Windows so far, with most of its protection, such as Windows **Defender**'s anti-spyware and Windows **Firewall**, working unobtrusively in the background. It is best to sign in or create a **Live** account to get Windows security from **www.windowsdefender.com**.

Windows 8 also supports multi-touch screens, handwriting and voice, but one needs suitable hardware to use these.

Versions

Windows 8 is available in four new versions – three of which are for the Intel and AMD PCs; Windows 8 (I'll call it Basic to distinguish it from the more general term for Windows 8), Windows 8 Pro and Windows 8 Enterprise and one, Windows RT, which will only run on ARM processors, allowing for more integration with the tablet market. However only the first three of these can be bought as the Windows 8 RT version will only be available pre-installed on new devices with ARM processors and will include touch-optimised desktop versions of Microsoft Word, Excel, PowerPoint and OneNote – it cannot be bought separately.

If your current machine runs Windows 7 Starter, Home Basic or Home Premium, you can upgrade to Windows 8 (Basic) or Windows 8 Pro. However, those on Windows 7 Professional or Windows 7 Ultimate will be able to Upgrade only to Windows 8 Pro. Clients on Microsoft's Assurance licensing agreements will be able to upgrade to Windows 8 Enterprise, but this is of no concern to most of us.

In short, owners of Intel and AMD PCs, laptops or tablets with x86 or x64 processor will be able to choose between Windows 8 (Basic) and Windows 8 Pro. Windows 8 Pro offers several features including encryption, PC management, virtualisation and domain connectivity. So the choice is really made for you, particularly if you want to install Windows **Media Center** which is only available to Windows 8 Pro as a separate 'media pack'.

Windows 8 (meaning both Basic and Pro) will run all your programs that currently run on Windows 7 or Windows Vista and you can perform an in-situ upgrade retaining all your files and settings. Upgrading from Windows XP requires an entirely new (clean) installation which means that anything not backed-up will be lost!

Finally, Windows 8 allows dual installation which you can choose during the Setup by selecting the 'Customised' install. In this way you can try the new Windows environment before you commit yourself fully!

System Requirements

To run Windows 8 a PC requires at least:

- A processor with a speed of 1 GHz or faster
- Available RAM: 1 GB (gigabyte) for a 32-bit (x86) system or 2 GB for a 64-bit (x64) system
- A graphics card that is DirectX 9 compatible with a WDDM 1.0 or higher driver
- 20 GB of available hard disc space.

To use all of Windows 8's features you will also need:

- To access the Internet, get mail or download and run Apps from Windows Apps Store, you need an active Internet connection and a minimum screen resolution of 1024 x 768.
- To use Windows Touch, you need a Tablet with an ARM processor or a monitor that supports multi-touch.
- Depending on resolution, video playback may require additional memory and advanced graphics hardware.
- HomeGroup requires a network and PCs running Windows 8.

Upgrading to Windows 8

If your computer operates under Windows 7, then it will run under Windows 8 without any problems. Windows 8 comes either as a 32-bit or a 64-bit Operating System (OS), with separate discs for the two versions. To use the 64-bit OS you will require a 64-bit computer, so be careful. If you need to find out which type of computer you have, check in the **System** section of the **Control Panel** which in Windows 7 is reached through the **Start** ● button.

You will also have to decide whether to do:

- An **Upgrade** – which replaces Windows 7 (or Vista) with Windows 8 and retains all your settings, data files and programs, or

- A **Custom** installation – after backing-up your settings and data files carry out a clean install. This cures the gradual slowdown that tends to happen to most PCs over time and cleans your PC of any bugs it might have picked up from the Internet. But, the downside is that you'll have to reinstall all your programs! With Windows XP you'll have to do a clean install.

Whichever installation you do, it is always a good idea to backup your settings and data files before installing a new operating system.

Before Installing Windows 8

To save time and help avoid problems during a Windows 8 installation, you should:

- Plug in and switch on all the peripheral devices you will be using with Windows 8.

- Connect to the Internet. This way you will get the latest installation updates, including security and hardware driver updates that can help with the installation.

- Sign in or create a new Windows **Live** account as the password is used by Windows 8 whenever you start the program – if you don't have a **Live** account, go to http://download.live.com/ to download **Live Essentials**.

Having obtained a Windows **Live** account, you can now proceed with the Windows 8 installation, following the instructions given on screen. If all is well, you'll just have to be patient now as this type of installation takes some considerable time (depending on your system) and your PC will reboot a number of times before installation is completed. At some point you'll be asked to input your product key which is usually on a label on the Windows 8 packaging.

If you choose to install Windows 8 on a partitioned drive, so as to retain Windows 7, then a dual boot will be required by changing a setting in the computer's basic input/output system (or BIOS).

How to do this varies with different manufacturers. Usually, you press a key (such as **F2** or **F12**) immediately after turning on your computer and before Windows starts. When the BIOS setup screen appears in black and white, select the **Boot order option** (or something similar), select the partition drive letter onto which you intend to install Windows 8 as the second startup device, save the setting changes, and then exit the BIOS. This may sound a bit heavy but if you take your time it should be no problem.

Installing Windows 8

Turn on your computer so that Windows starts normally, open the DVD drive and insert the Windows 8 installation disc. When you close the DVD drive, the Windows Setup should start. On the **Which type of installation do you want?** page, click:

- **Upgrade** if you are upgrading from Windows 7 and want to retain your files and settings, or

- **Custom**, only if you are installing on a partition drive and you want to retain your Windows 7 version. In the **where do you want to install Windows?** page, select **Drive options (advanced)** and select the partition that you want to install Windows 8, then just follow the instructions to finish the installation.

You will be asked to name your computer and use your Windows **Live** user account.

The Windows.old Folder

If you delete or format a partition that contains a version of Windows, all the data on the partition is permanently deleted.

However, if there is an existing copy of Windows on the partition you selected (as it would be if you are upgrading), and you don't format or delete the partition, your user files will be saved to a **windows.old** folder on that partition (usually C:), which you can browse after the installation completes. This is a safety net, so that if anything goes wrong you could restored your files after installing Windows 8.

If all is well, however, it is recommended that you delete the **windows.old** folder, as the amount of data stored in the folder can be very large, thus reducing your available disc space.

Anti-virus Software

You should now have a running version of Windows 8 to play with, but before you do anything else you should reinstall your anti-virus software. Without it you would be very vulnerable on the Internet.

If you don't have any and you don't want to pay for this, you can download excellent free anti-virus and anti-spyware protection at:

www.windowsdefender.com

or

www.free.avg.com

I have used both of these on some of my computers for many years and found them excellent. For more information on Windows Defender, please refer to Chapter 13.

How to install programs in Windows 8 will become very clear once Windows 8 is up and running, as described in the next chapter.

2

Starting Windows 8

The Windows 8 Desktop

When you first switch on your tablet or PC a screen similar to that in Fig. 2.1 appears on your display, known as the **Lock** screen. Swiping upwards on the **Lock** screen or dragging the mouse pointer upwards, displays a second screen in which you enter your user details after which Windows 8 opens with the Modern interface displaying the distinctive tiled Apps screen shown for my version in Fig. 2.2 on the next page.

6:12
Monday, October 29

Fig. 2.1 A Windows 8 Opening Screen.

Note: Most swipe movements of your finger on a multi-touch screen correspond to dragging the mouse pointer on a PC. Similarly, tapping on such touch-screen devices corresponds to clicking the left mouse button. Touch and hold corresponds to a right-click of the mouse button. For more details, please refer to Appendix A.

Fig. 2.2 The Tiled Apps in Windows 8.

The display shown in Fig. 2.2 is the tiled **Start** screen, with tiles grouped into three columns. On the first two columns are all the pre-installed Apps to access **Mail**, **Internet Explorer**, **Store**, **Calendar, Maps**, **SkyDrive**, **Bing**, etc. while the third column displays shortcuts to any programs you might have installed yourself or were retained after upgrading. Tapping or left-clicking any of these tiles, starts the App or program.

Tapping or clicking the **Desktop** tile shown at the bottom-left corner of the **Start** screen in Fig. 2.2 above, opens the Windows 8 **Desktop** shown in Fig. 2.3.

Fig. 2.3 The Windows 8 Desktop.

To toggle between the **Desktop** or an App screen and the **Start** screen, click the bottom-left corner of the **Desktop** screen to reveal a thumbnail of the **Start** screen, as shown in Fig. 2.3 on the previous page. Left-clicking this, opens the tiled **Start** screen. Alternatively, press the **Windows** 🔲 key on the keyboard to do the same thing.

The Taskbar

The thumbnail of the **Start** screen in Fig. 2.3, obscures the left most part of the **Taskbar** which is situated at the bottom of the **Desktop** screen, as shown separately in Fig. 2.4 below.

   Fig. 2.4 The Internet Explorer and
File Explorer Buttons.

To the right of the **Taskbar** you'll find the **Notification Area**, which includes a Digital clock as shown in Fig. 2.5 below.

Fig. 2.5 The Notification Area.

Tapping or clicking the **Date/Time** display area in Fig. 2.5 above, opens the screen shown in Fig. 2.6 below and selecting the **Change date and time settings** link, displays a tabbed dialogue box in which you can change the date and time, time zone and add two additional clocks. This can be very useful if you have friends living at different time zones and want to avoid waking them up!

Below we show the display when you tap or click the **Date/Time** area after adding two more clocks to the local time.

Fig. 2.6 The Change Date and
Time Screen.

With this version of Windows, only programs that you chose to pin to the **Taskbar** appear on it, as shown in Fig. 2.7.

 Fig. 2.7 Windows 8 Taskbar Pinned Program Buttons.

In this case the **Internet Explorer** button in Fig. 2.7 appears as if there is another button hiding behind it. By placing a finger or the mouse pointer on it, thumbnails are displayed showing the opened **Explorer** tabs, as shown in Fig. 2.8. This can also happen with other running items.

Fig. 2.8 Thumbnails Showing Open Internet Explorer Tabs.

As you can see, there were two tabs open in **Explorer** and each is shown as a thumbnail. Moving the mouse pointer over a thumbnail temporarily displays that window full size on the screen so you can see in more detail what it contains. At the same time, a **Close** 🗙 button appears on the top-right hand side of the thumbnail. Tapping or clicking a thumbnail will open the **Explorer** tab with that view active, while tapping or clicking the **Close** button will close that tab. **Internet Explorer** behaves the same if opened from the tiled **Start** screen.

Running Apps

Apps you have accessed during a session continue running until you close them. To see which Apps are running, place the mouse pointer at the bottom-left corner of the screen so that the thumbnail of the **Start** screen appears, then drag the pointer upwards to display a screen similar to that of Fig. 2.9 on the next page.

Fig. 2.9 The Thumbnails of Running Apps.

So now you can access any of these running Apps by tapping or clicking on its thumbnail. You can also force an App to close (stop running) by either right-clicking on the App and selecting **Close** from the displayed menu or dragging the open App from the very top of the screen towards the bottom with either the mouse or your finger, as shown below.

Fig. 2.10 Closing Apps.

Pined programs on the **Taskbar** can be run by just tapping or clicking on their button. To stop a running program, tap or click the **Close** ☒ button that appears on the top-right hand side of its open window or on its thumbnail, if not opened on the screen.

To pin a running program on the **Taskbar** right-click its image on the **Taskbar** and select the **Pin this program to taskbar** option, as shown here in Fig. 2.11.

Fig. 2.11 The Right-click Options of a Running Program.

Status Buttons on the Notification Area

On the **Notification** area, also called the **System Tray**, on the right of the **Taskbar** that includes the digital clock and date, you'll find other icons showing the status of the **Action Center** 🖳, power 🔋 (for a laptop), network 🖧 (Ethernet) or 📶 (wireless), and the volume setting of your speakers 🔊. Other application icons are hidden by default and their notifications are suppressed.

When you point to an icon, an information bubble opens showing the status for that setting as shown here.

However, tapping or clicking the **Network** icon 🖧, or 📶, for instance, displays more detailed information about whether you are connected and to which network, as shown in Fig. 2.12.

Try tapping or clicking the **Volume** icon 🔊 to open the volume controls so you can control the loudness of the speakers attached to your PC, or built into your laptop.

Tapping or clicking the **Action Center** icon 🖳 gives you a quick view of the status of your PC (Fig. 2.13).

Fig. 2.12 Available Networks.

If any problems are shown, you can tap or click the **Open Action Center** link to find out what they are and hopefully how you can solve them.

By default, Windows places any other icons in a 'hidden' area, but you can tap/click the **Show hidden icons** button 🔼 to temporarily show them again as shown here. You can control which icons appear on your **System Tray** by using the **Customize** link.

Fig. 2.13 The Action Center.

The Charms Bar

Charms provide a quick and easy access to a wide range of options from either the **Start** screen or Apps screens. To access these, either point with the mouse at the top-right corner of the screen or swipe from the right edge of the screen towards the left to reveal the **Charms**. As you move the mouse pointer downwards towards the **Charms**, they display within a dark bar as shown in Fig. 2.14.

The first of these is used to **Search** for Apps, settings and specific files. It can also be used to search within a running App. The **Share** allows you to share content, while the **Start** displays the **Start** screen and from there toggles to the **Desktop** view. The **Devices** charm displays such peripherals as a secondary screen, while **Settings** allows you to change the settings within Windows 8, as well as powering off (shutting down) your PC or device.

Fig. 2.14.

Ending a Session

When you have finished for the day, it is important to save your work and 'turn off' your PC or tablet properly, both to protect your data and to save energy. With Windows 8 there

are several options for ending the session, all available from the **Power** button of the **Settings** charm as shown in Fig. 2.15 (see also Appendix B). If you are the sole user of your computer, only the three displayed options are available; **Sleep**, **Shut down** or **Restart**. Other options are displayed once there are more family members sharing the same computer.

Fig. 2.15 Shut Down Options.

From here you can select to put the computer in **Sleep** mode, **Shut Down** it down completely or **Restart** it to clear the memory settings and reset Windows.

Selecting the **Sleep** option or closing the lid of a laptop puts the computer to **Sleep** and turns the display and fan off. A light on the outside of the case blinks to indicate that the computer is asleep and the whole process takes only a few seconds.

When you turn the PC back on or open the lid of a laptop, the same **Lock** screen as if you just started your computer displays (see Fig. 2.1). You will need to swipe or drag the mouse pointer upwards to reveal the screen where you enter your password. After providing your password, the screen will look exactly as it did before you put your device to **Sleep** with all your running Apps in place. The advantage of the **Sleep** mode is that because you don't have to wait for Windows to start, you can resume work almost immediately.

By default, selecting the **Shut down** option turns the computer completely off, while the **Restart** option clears your computer's memory settings and resets Windows. Sometimes when you select either the **Shut down** or the **Restart** option, Windows installs any updates first, if available, before carrying on with the selected option.

Note: It is important to let Windows install its updates, even if you are in the middle of doing something else. Far too many users who skip this process, find themselves in trouble later. Updates are not there to annoy you, they are there to protect you!

3

The Windows 8 Settings

User Accounts

What is shown in Fig. 3.1 is a composite of two screens; the **Charms** bar options on the right of the display and what you will see to the left of it, if you tap or click the **Setting** charm.

If you are not sure how to display the **Charms** bar, please refer to the end of the previous chapter.

Tapping or clicking the **Change PC settings** link, pointed to at the bottom of the **Settings** screen, displays a new screen as shown in Fig. 3.2 on the next page with the **Users** option open.

Windows allows for several people (like a family) to share a computer, with each having their own set-up, by using individual **User Accounts**. Each account tells Windows what files and folders the holder can access, what changes can be made to the computer and controls their personal preferences.

Fig. 3.1 A Windows 8 Opening Screen.

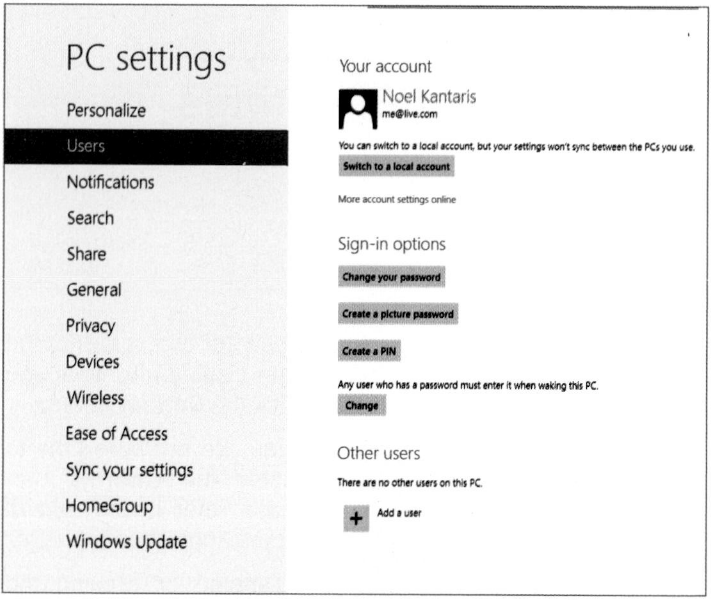

Fig. 3.2 The Windows 8 Users Settings Screen.

To add a user, simply tap or click the **Add a user** button at the bottom of the screen to display the screen in Fig. 3.3 and supply the appropriate information – it is that simple!

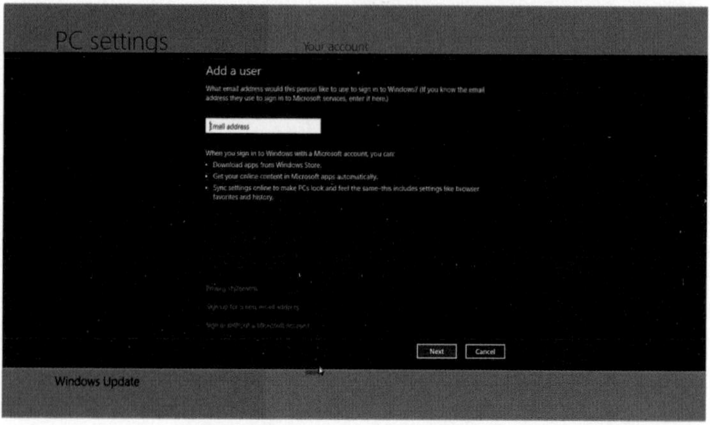

Fig. 3.3 The Add a User Screen.

Personalising your PC

On the **Settings** screen in Fig. 3.2, selecting the first listed option opens the screen shown in Fig. 3.4 below.

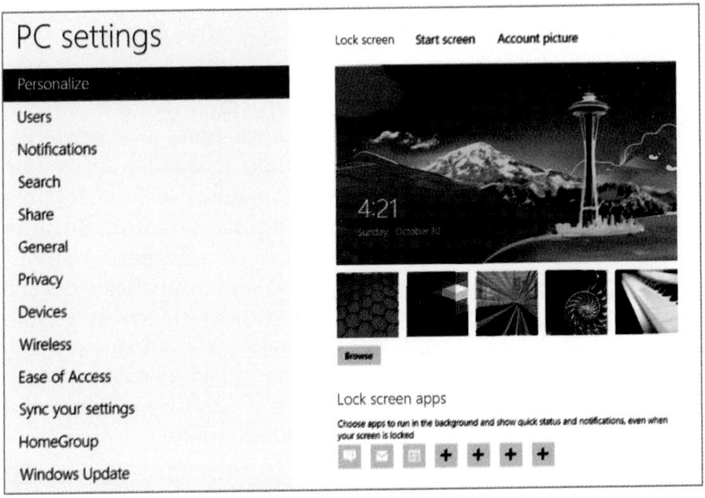

Fig. 3.4 The Windows Personalise Settings Screen.

From here you can change the **Lock** screen (the first screen you see when you start Windows) to one of the alternatives shown or you can browse though your pictures to choose one of your own.

You can also change the **Start** screen and its colour, as well as your account picture. When you select this last option you are given the opportunity to use the camera on your PC to take your picture there and then!

Finally, you can also choose which Apps should run in the background and give you up-to-date information. There are already some Apps preselected, but you can add to these by tapping or clicking the ✚ button.

Do try the various listed options under the **PC Settings** before you leave this section – have a look and find out what is on offer.

Windows Themes

Another way of personalising your screen is with the

selection of themes which you can find in the **Personalization** option on the **Settings** screen. In Fig. 3.5 only the top of the screen is shown.

Fig. 3.5 The Windows Personalization Option.

Selecting this option, displays the screen shown in Fig. 3.6 below. Plenty to explore here! For example, you can change (please refer to the bottom of the screen in Fig. 3.6) the **Desktop** background, **Color**, **Sounds** and choose a **Screen Saver**. Windows 8 comes with three default **Themes** which include most of the above changes at once, namely **Windows** (the best choice), **Earth** and **Flowers**. You can also get additional themes online.

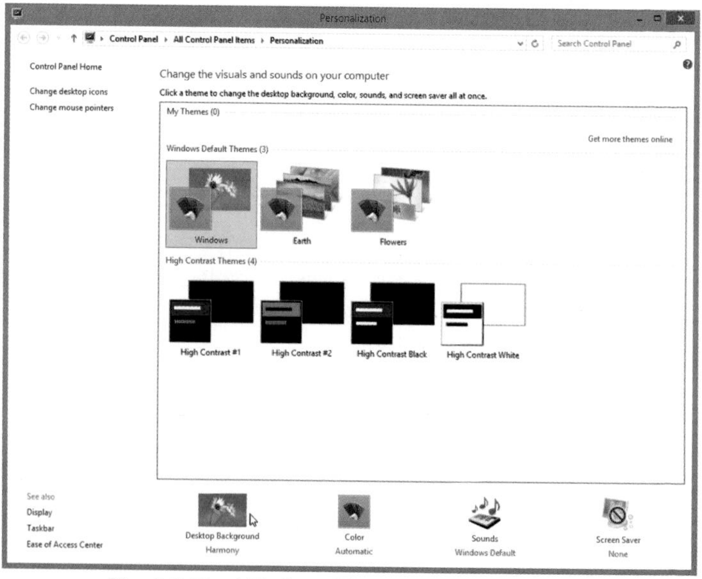

Fig. 3.6 The Windows Themes Settings Screen.

Selecting a Screen Saver

You can use the **Screen Saver** link in the **Personalization** window (Fig. 3.6) to open the screen shown in Fig. 3.7 below.

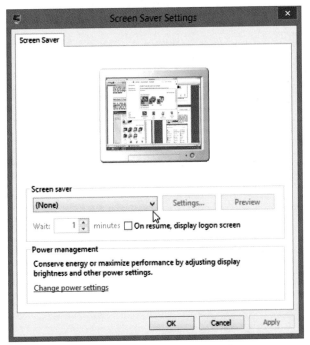

Fig. 3.7 The Screen Saver Settings Screen.

Tapping or clicking the down-arrow on the **Screen saver** box reveals a drop-down menu of the installed screen savers you can choose from, but it depends on personal preferences.

In this window you can also change the time of inactivity before the screen saver starts up. With some screen savers, clicking the **Settings** button displays a box for you to control their display settings. When you make all the changes you want, tap or click the **Preview** button to see the effect of the selected options in full screen. When you are happy, stop the preview, then tap or click the **Apply** button followed by the **OK** button.

Controlling your System

The main way of controlling your computer (PC or tablet), is through the **Control Panel** which provides quick and easy ways to change the hardware and software settings of your system. You can access the **Control Panel** either through the entry on the **Settings** screen (Fig. 3.5) or the link provided on the **Personalization** screen in Fig. 3.6. Either way opens the screen shown in Fig. 3.8 below.

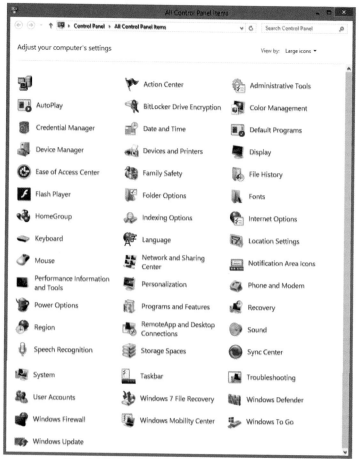

Fig. 3.8 The Windows Control Panel Screen.

From here you can add new hardware, remove or change programs, change the display type and its resolution, control your computer's setup and security, and a lot more besides. However daunting this may look, it is a very good idea to get familiar with the **Control Panel** features. Once you know your way around it, you can set up Windows just the way it suits you. The actual options available in **Control Panel** depend on your computer hardware and your version of Windows 8.

Changing the Windows Display

Display   Windows 8 requires the highest possible screen resolution that your graphics card is capable of delivering so that it can give you better text clarity, sharper images, and fit more items on your screen. At lower resolutions, less items fit on the screen, and images may have jagged edges. For example, a display resolution of 1024 x 768 pixels (picture elements) is low, while 1600 x 900 pixels, or higher, is better.

Whether you can increase your screen resolution depends on the size and capability of your monitor and the type of video card installed in your system. To find out if you can increase the display resolution, use the **Display** icon in **Control** (shown above), to open the **Display** screen, then select the **Adjust resolution** link, to open the screen below.

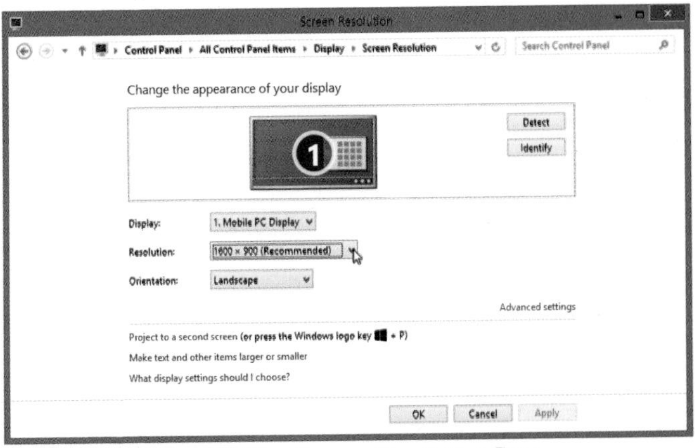

Fig. 3.9 The Screen Resolution Box.

Tapping or clicking the down arrow to the right of the resolution box, opens a drop-down box similar to the one shown in Fig. 3.10, with your monitor's resolution settings and capabilities. It is best to select the highest possible resolution available.

Fig. 3.10 The Windows Display Resolution.

From the display in Fig. 3.9, you can also arrange to **Project to a second screen**, if you have a larger monitor connected to your system.

Controlling Devices and Printers

When your computer was first set up, your devices and printers should have been installed automatically. If not, select the **Devices and Printers** icon (shown above) from the **Control Panel** to open the screen shown in Fig. 3.11 below.

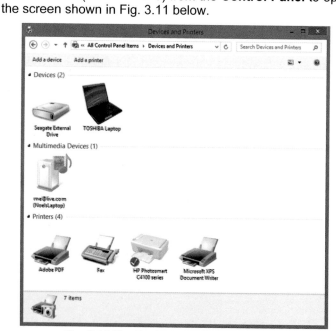

Fig. 3.11 The Devices and Printers Screen.

My **Devices and Printers** screen displays two devices, one multimedia device and four printers, one of which is a Fax. In the case of the printers, one is physical for printing to paper and two for creating formatted print (Adobe PDF and Microsoft XPS) documents.

With Windows 8, most devices and printers are automatically detected at installation time, or during the boot-up process. So if you add a new printer or a new device, like a camera, to your system it should be recognised. You may be asked for the necessary driver files if they are not already in the Windows directory, but these come on a CD, or can be found on the manufacturer's Web site.

Configuring your Printer

To control your printer, tap or click its icon in the **Devices and Printers** screen (Fig. 3.11), to open a 'Printer Control' window like that shown in Fig. 3.12 below.

Fig. 3.12 The Printer Control Window.

From here you can control what is waiting to be printed and customise paper orientation. Other device options specific to the printer might also display.

A newly installed printer is automatically set as the default printer, indicated by a green ✅ tick against it in the **Devices and Printers** screen. To change the default printer, select a printer connected to your PC, touch and hold or right-click it, and choose the **Set as default printer** option from the drop-down menu.

Once you have installed and configured your printers, the quickest way to print a simple document or file is to print using Windows itself. Locate the file that you want to print in a folder, maybe **Documents**, touch and hold or right-click it, and select **Print** from the displayed menu. Windows will print it using your default printer settings.

Managing Print Jobs

If you want to find out what is happening when you have sent documents to your printer, double-tap or double-click the **See what's printing** option in the **Printer Control** window, or double-tap/click the printer icon 🖶 in the **Notification Area** of the **Taskbar**, to open the **Print Queue**.

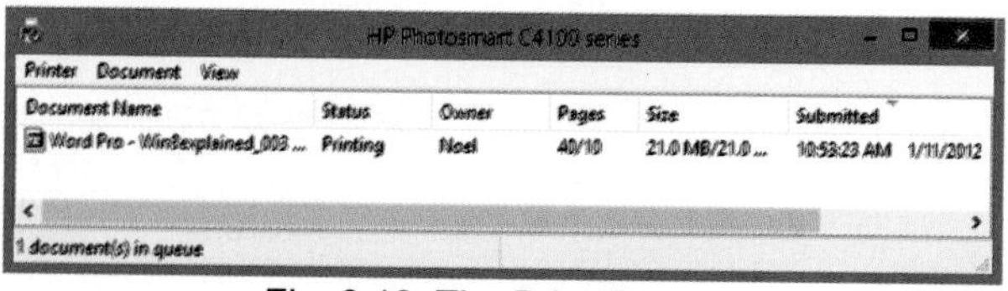

Fig. 3.13 The Print Queue.

This displays detailed information about the work actually being printed, or of print jobs that are waiting in the queue. This includes the name of the document, its status and 'owner', when it was added to the print queue, the printing progress and when printing was started.

You can control the printing operations from the **Printer** and **Document** menu options of the **Print Queue** window. Selecting **Printer**, **Pause Printing** will stop the operation until you make the same selection again. The **Cancel All Documents** option will remove all the print jobs from the queue, but it sometimes takes a while. If an error occurs with a print job, it will be necessary to use the **Cancel All Documents** option, before you can print anything else.

Working with Programs

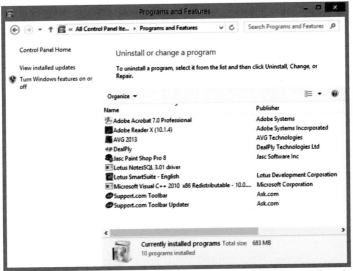

Installing programs on your computer is very easy with Windows 8. Just place the CD or DVD that the software came on in the appropriate drive and Windows will start the installation process automatically. If you downloaded the program from the Internet, it should run and install itself. Use the **Programs and Features** icon on the **Control Panel** (shown above), to open the screen shown in Fig. 3.14. Your contents will not be the same, obviously!

Fig. 3.14 The Programs and Features screen of the Control Panel.

Uninstalling or Changing a Program

Uninstalling programs or changing an already installed one is very easy with Windows. To do either, select the program you want to work with. After selecting a program, three extra options may appear after **Organize**; namely, **Uninstall**, **Change**, and **Repair**. However, with some programs **Change** and/or **Repair** are not available, while with others **Change** is replaced by the **Repair** option only.

Using the option to **Uninstall** a program, removes all trace of it from your hard disc, although sometimes the folders are left empty on your hard drive.

> **Note:** Be careful with this application, because selecting a program on the list might remove it without further warning!

Running a Program as Administrator

If a program that you are trying to run gives you errors such as **Access Denied** or **No Permission**, then running it as an administrator can usually give the permission it needs to run properly. With Windows, an administrator is someone allowed to make changes on a computer that will affect other users. These include security settings, installing software and hardware, and being able to access all files on the computer.

Somewhat confusingly even if your account is set up as an **Administrator** you will still be prompted to give 'Administrator' rights at certain times. There is a 'Hidden Administrator' account with full powers over your computer and this is the one you sometimes have to access.

> **Note:** You should only allow a program that you trust to run as administrator as once you have given full permission, it will have complete access to your computer.

If you are doing this while logged in as a standard user instead of an administrator, then you will need to provide the administrator's password before the program will run as administrator.

4

The Desktop File Explorer

 If you have used Windows 7 and Office 2010 (or Office 2007), you'll be familiar with the **File Explorer** (the old Windows Explorer), in which case you could skip this chapter. If, on the other hand you did not have this experience, read on!

File Explorer's Libraries

In Windows 8 every user starts with their own Apps, programs and a set of data folders called simply **Documents**, **Pictures**, **Music** and **Videos** stored in **Libraries**. To see your **Libraries**, tap or click the **File Explorer** button on the **Taskbar** to open the **Libraries** window similar to that in Fig. 4.1.

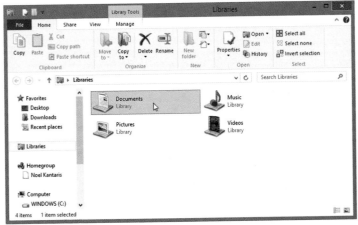

Fig. 4.1 A Set of Personal Libraries.

Libraries, although not folders themselves, can point to different folders on your hard disc, or on an external drive attached to your computer. They let you quickly access files from multiple folders without moving them from their original location. For example, say you have video files on both your hard disc and on an external drive, you can now access all of your video files from the **Videos** library. How to do that will be discussed at the end of this chapter.

The left pane of the **Libraries** window, called the **Navigation** pane, lists your **Favorites** and gives you access to tree-style views of your **Libraries**, your **HomeGroup**, your **Computer**, and your **Network**.

The right pane of the **Libraries** window lists the folders and files in the selected location. Tapping or clicking a link in the **Navigation** pane opens its contents in the right pane.

Folders are just containers in which you can store files or other folders. Arranging files into logical groups in folders makes it easier to locate and work with them. For example in Fig. 4.2 below, folders are shown for one of my drives.

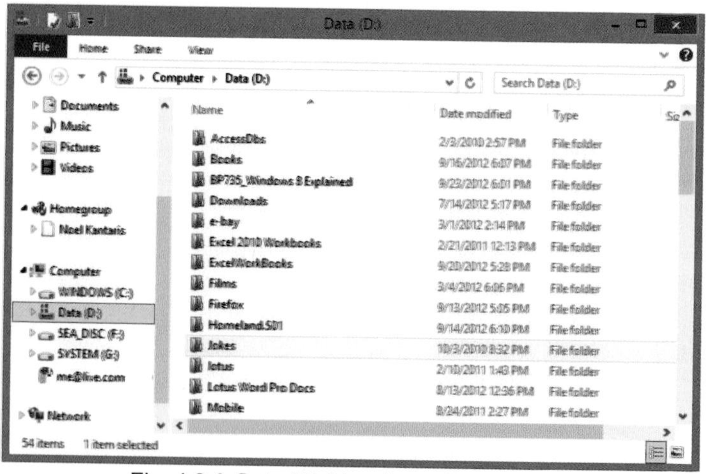

Fig. 4.2 A Set of Folders in my Data Drive.

Double-tapping or double-clicking a folder opens it and displays its contents as shown in Fig. 4.3 on the next page.

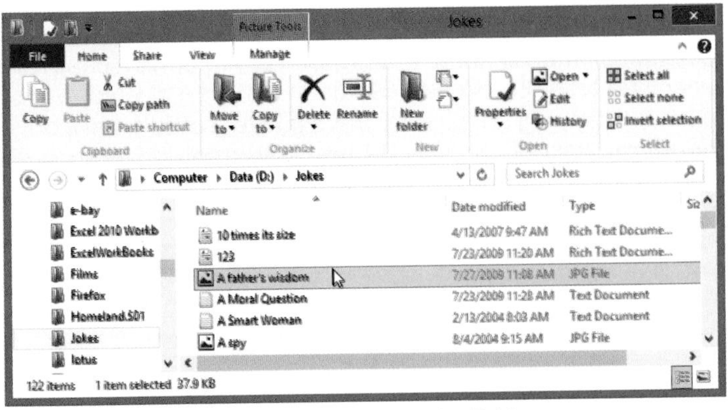

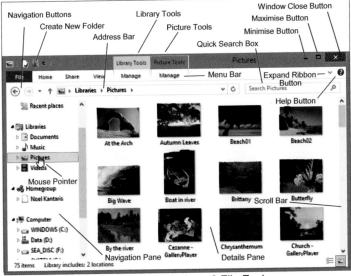

Fig. 4.3 The Contents of a Folder.

Files contain related information, such as a word-processed letter, a digital photo, a spreadsheet, a video or a music track.

Parts of a Window

In Fig. 4.4, a typical Windows 8 **File Explorer** window is shown with its constituent parts labelled and later described.

Fig. 4.4 Parts of a Windows 8 File Explorer.

You may have noticed by now that the buttons on the toolbars of the different **File Explorer** windows change to reflect the type of work you can do in that type of window. For example, tapping or clicking the **Picture Tools** label above the **Menu bar**, displays a **Ribbon** with appropriate tools to **Edit** or **View** pictures, as shown in Fig. 4.5. The **Ribbon** will be discussed shortly.

Fig. 4.5 The Picture Tools Ribbon.

Once you open one **Ribbon** or used the **Expand Ribbon** ⌄ button (see Fig. 4.4 for its location), then tapping or clicking each **Menu** bar option (apart from **File**), displays different but appropriate ribbons allowing you to work with the selected option. You can close the **Ribbon** by tapping or clicking the **Minimise Ribbon** ⌃ button which replaces the **Expand Ribbon** ⌄ button, once the ribbon has been expanded.

The typical **File Explorer** window is subdivided into several areas which have the following functions:

Area	*Function*
Minimise button	Tapping or clicking the **Minimise** button stores a window and its contents as an icon on the **Taskbar**. Clicking on such an icon will restore the window
Maximise button	Tapping or clicking the **Maximise** button fills the screen with the active window. When that happens, the **Maximise** button changes to a **Restore Down** button which can be used to restore the window to its former size.
Close button	The extreme top right button that you tap or click to close a window.

Navigation buttons	The **Go Back** (left) button takes you to the previous display, while the **Go Forward** (right) button takes you to the next display. The down-arrow ▼ gives access to **Recent Locations**.
↑	Tapping or clicking this button takes you one level up towards the **Desktop**.
Address bar	Shows the location of the current folder. You can change locations here, or switch to an **Internet Explorer** window by typing a Web address.
Quick search box	The box in which you type your search criteria. As you start typing, the displayed files filter down to just the matching terms, making it much easier to find your files.
Menu bar	The bar allows you to choose from several menu options. Tapping or clicking on a menu item displays the pull-down menu associated with it.
Toolbar	A bar of icons that you tap or click to carry out some common actions (see Fig. 4.5). The icons displayed depend on the type of window.
Scroll bars/buttons	The bars/buttons at the extreme right and bottom of each window (or pane within a window) that contain a scroll box/button. Tapping or clicking on these, allows you to see parts of a document that might not be visible in that size window.
Mouse pointers	The arrow which appears when the pointer is placed over menus, scroll bars, buttons and lists or the hand that displays when pointing to a link.

The File Menu Bar Option

Tapping or clicking the **File** option on a window's menu bar, displays a screen similar to the one shown in Fig. 4.6. In this case the **Help** option was selected to show you where to find it. Each listed option under **File** displays different options in the **Details** pane.

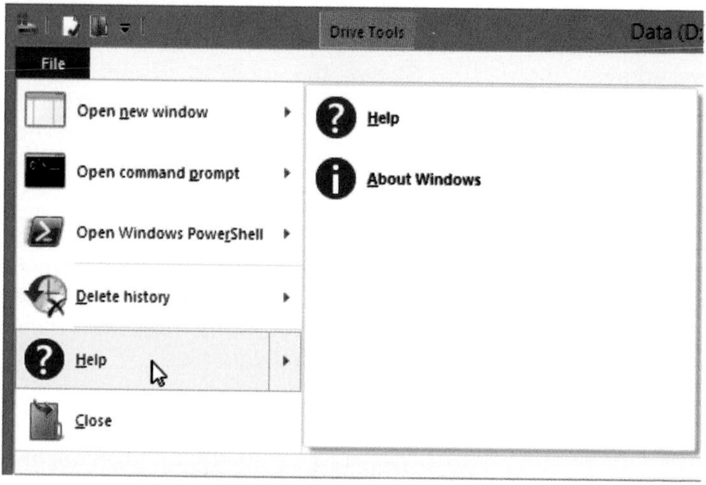

Fig. 4.6 The File Menu Option.

Items on the sub-menu marked with an arrow to their right ▶, open up additional options when selected.

> **Note:** Having activated the **File** menu, you can close it without taking any further action by simply tapping or clicking outside its window, or by pressing the **Esc** key on the keyboard. If you select the **Close** option instead, you will exit the **File Explorer** altogether.

Manipulating Windows

To use any Windows program effectively, including the **File Explorer**, you need to be able to move a window or re-size it so that you can see all of it.

Changing the active window – If you have several windows open on the screen, you can make one active by simply tapping or clicking it or, if it is not visible, tap or click its icon on the **Taskbar**. In the case of running Apps, point at the bottom-left corner of the screen with the mouse so that the thumbnail of the **Start** screen appears, then drag upwards to display them and click on the one you want. Swiping with your finger from the left edge of the screen towards the middle, displays open Apps in rotation.

Moving a window – To move a window, point to its **Title** bar with either your finger or the mouse, and drag it until it is where you want on the screen. You can only do this if the window does not occupy the full screen and it has a maximise button 🔲 visible.

Minimising and maximising windows – To minimise a window into a **Taskbar** icon, tap or click the **Minimize** button ▬ in the upper-right corner of the window. To maximise a window so that it fills the entire screen, tap or click the **Maximize** button 🔲, or double-tap or double-click in the **Title** bar. Double-tapping/clicking again will restore it.

A window that has been minimised or maximised can be returned to its original size and position on the screen by either tapping or clicking on its **Taskbar** icon to expand it to a window, or tapping or clicking on the **Restore Down** button 🔲 of a maximised window, to reduce it to its former size.

 Re-sizing a window – To change the size of a window either place your finger on a visible edge of the window, or corner, and drag the edge or corner to the required place. With the mouse, the pointer first changes to a two-headed arrow when placed at the edge or corner, as shown here, before you can drag.

Closing a window – To close a window and save screen space and memory, tap or click the **Close** button ▬ ✕ ▬.

Additional Sizing Features

Windows 8 also includes some additional ways to manipulate windows. These can be carried out using a mouse or your finger if you have touch-sensitive hardware.

Maximising windows – To maximise the current window, you drag its **Title** bar up towards the top of the screen. When the cursor touches the top of the screen, the window will maximise.

Snapping windows to the edge of the screen – This allows the display of two windows side by side (each taking half the width of your screen, as shown in Fig. 4.7.

Fig. 4.7 Two Windows Displaying Side-by-side.

To achieve this, drag one window to the left by its **Title** bar. When the cursor hits the left side of the screen, the window will snap to that edge and re-size to occupy the left half of the screen. Next, drag a second window to the right by its **Title** bar. When the cursor hits the screen edge, the window will re-size and snap to the right half of the screen.

Restoring a maximised or snapped window – Drag the window by its **Title** bar, back towards the centre of the screen and it will return to its previous size and position.

The Ribbon

Traditional menus and toolbars in **File Explorer** have been replaced by the **Ribbon** – a device that presents commands organised into a set of tabs, as shown in Fig.4.8.

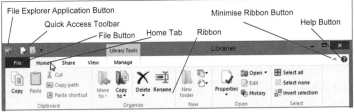

Fig. 4.8 The Home Tab of the File Explorer Ribbon.

The tabs on the **Ribbon** display the commands that are most relevant for each of the task areas in a **Library** activity (in this case), as shown above for **File Explorer**.

Note the **Minimise the Ribbon** ⌃ button which you tap or click to gain more space on your screen. It then changes to the **Expand the Ribbon** ⌄ button, which you tap or click to display the **Ribbon** again.

Also note that there are three basic components to the Ribbon, as shown in Fig. 4.9 below.

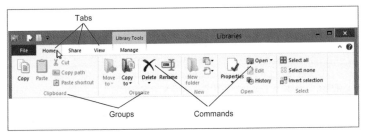

Fig. 4.9 The Components of the Ribbon.

The Ribbon Components are:

Tabs   There are several basic tabs across the top, each representing an activity area.

Groups   Each tab has several groups that show related items together.

Commands   A command can be a button or a box to read or enter information.

For each activity the **Home** tab contains all the things you use most often, such as creating a **New** folder, the **Copy** and **Delete** commands, etc. Tapping or clicking a new tab opens a new series of groups, each with its relevant command buttons. This really works very well.

Contextual tabs also appear, as we have seen earlier, when they are needed so that you can very easily find and use the commands needed for the current operation.

Below the content of the other three **Ribbon** tabs is displayed.

Fig. 4.10 The Share Tab of the File Explorer Ribbon.

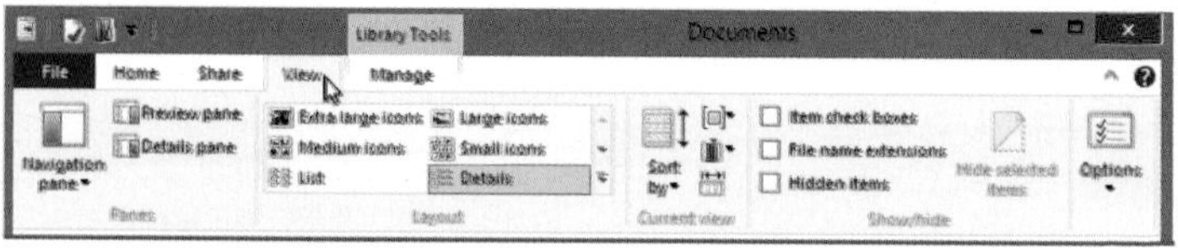

Fig. 4.11 The View Tab of the File Explorer Ribbon.

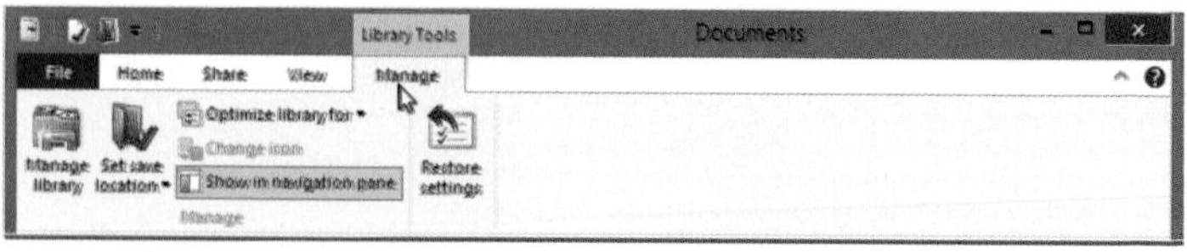

Fig. 4.12 The Manage Tab of the File Explorer Ribbon.

Adding Locations to the Library

To add a new location to a library, so that the contents of that location are available to the **Libraries**, tap or click on the required library entry, say the **Videos** library as an example, to open the screen shown in Fig. 4.13 below, with the **Manage** tab active.

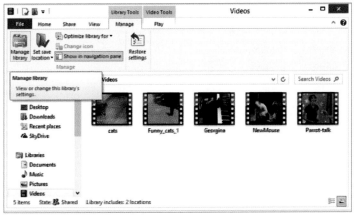

Fig. 4.13 The Manage Tab of the File Explorer Ribbon.

As you can see from the above screen, the **Videos** library already points to a videos folder which allows it to display the above screen. To add another location to the **Videos** library, such as a folder on another location on your hard disc

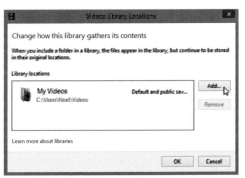

containing more videos, tap or click the **Manage library** option on the **Ribbon** (to be found under **File** in Fig. 4.13). This opens the screen shown here in Fig. 4.14.

Fig. 4.14 Adding a Videos Library Location.

Next, tap or click the **Add** button to open the display shown in Fig. 4.15 below.

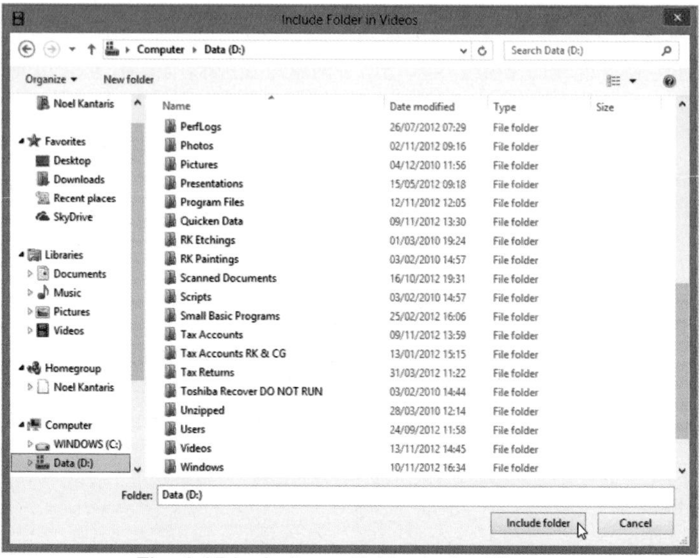

Fig. 4.15 Including a Folder to the Library.

On this screen you can locate the folder you want to include in your library, say a **Videos** folder either on another partition of your hard disc or additional hard disc, as shown above, select it and tap or click on the **Include folder** button.

You can apply this procedure to other **Libraries**, such as **Documents**, **Music** or **Pictures**. This is rather neat, I think!

5

The Internet Explorer

To start **Internet Explorer** from the **Desktop**, tap or click its icon ![] on the **Taskbar**, while to start it from the Windows **Start** screen, tap or click on its tile App pointed to in Fig. 5.1.

Fig. 5.1 The Windows Start Screen.

Either of these two actions opens the screen shown in Fig. 5.2, which displays a picture with **bing** (the Internet Search Engine) ready for you to enter your query in its search box.

Fig. 5.2 The Opening Explorer Screen.

The Bing Home Page Hotspots

You might have noticed that on the **bing Home** page there are small squares, called **Hotspots** which when you point to them display information on certain aspects of the view, as shown in Fig. 5.3 – a rather nice touch!

Fig. 5.3 The Windows Start Screen.

At the bottom of the screen, which changes its image daily, there is further information on the displayed picture, weather forecast and what is popular now in the news, as shown in Fig. 5.4.

Fig. 5.4 Further Points of Interest.

The two arrows (top-right on the above screen dump) can be used to go back to the previous day's picture or forward to the next day's picture.

The Bing Search Preferences

On the top-right of **bing**'s **Home** screen you'll find the **Preferences** button. Touching with your finger or clicking with the mouse, this button displays an **Internet Explorer** screen similar to that in Fig. 5.5 on the next page.

Note: There is a lot on this **Explorer** screen which you should open on your own monitor as it is impossible to enlarge it any further on the displayed screen dump. What is shown here is for the **General** preferences for **bing** with other screens available for **Web**, **Search History** and **Worldwide**. Do look at all of these and make any changes you need to, before using the Save button to make them permanent.

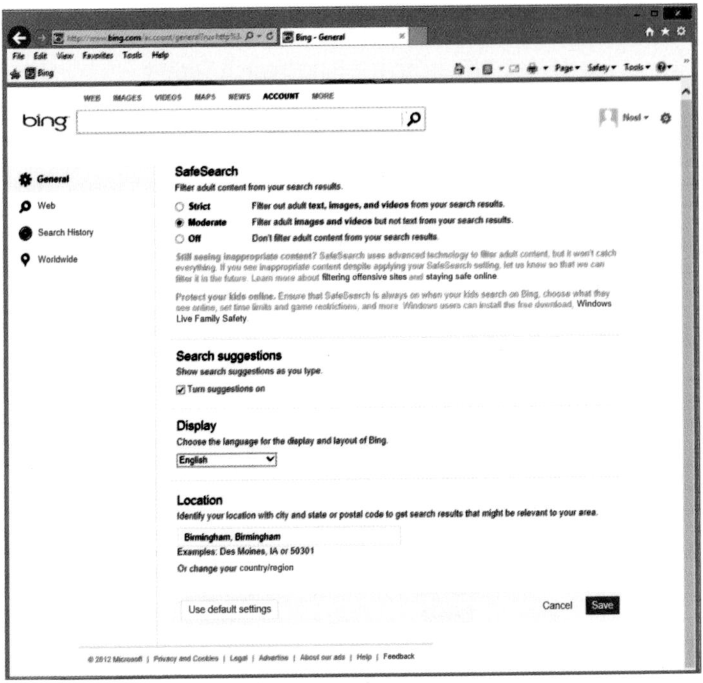

Fig. 5.5 The General Preferences Screen.

Searching the Web

In Fig. 5.6 below an enlarged **bing** search box is displayed.

Fig. 5.6 The Bing Search Box.

Note that you can specify that the results of your search should come **Only from the Unite Kingdom**, if that is what you want. However, before you type your query, have a look at the very top of the screen, shown enlarged in Fig. 5.7 on the next page.

| WEB | IMAGES   VIDEOS   MAPS   NEWS   SEARCH HISTORY   MORE | MSN | HOTMAIL

Fig. 5.7 The Top-left Bing Search Topics.

As you can see above, you can direct your search to specifics, such as the WEB (the default), IMAGES, VIDEOS, NEWS, etc. To search for pictures of Ely Cathedral, first select IMAGES, then in the screen of endless images displayed in **Internet Explorer**, type **Ely Cathedral** in the **Search** box. The result is shown enlarged in Fig. 5.8 below.

Fig. 5.8 Ely Cathedral in Pictures.

You can also search the VIDEOS option, where you'll find some very interesting videos of the cathedral. Before some videos start to play, an advert begins to display, which can be unexpected and, therefore, rather confusing. Luckily, you are given the choice to skip the advert.

If you exit **Internet Explorer** by starting another App, because you wanted to, say, check your mail, then selecting the **Explorer** tile again, will returned you to the exact screen you were looking at before you left it. You will be forgiven if you thought that there is no way out of this Web page!

To exit a Website, either type a new URL (Uniform Resource Locator) of a Web page in the **Address** bar, or grab the **Explorer** screen from the very top and drag it to the bottom of the screen. This last move also exits the **Explorer** all together. Next time you select its tile it will display **bing**.

The Address Bar

There are many millions of Web pages to look at on the Web, so where do you start? In **Internet Explorer** the **Address** bar is where you type or paste, the address or URL of a Web page you want to open.

For example, typing in the **Address** bar as shown in Fig. 5.9 and tapping or clicking the **Go to** button ➔ will open the list of books page on my personal Web site. Note that the **Go to** button then changes to the **Refresh** button ↻ which reloads the Web page shown in the **Address** bar when it is tapped or clicked.

![http://www.kantaris.com/noel/list.htm]

Fig. 5.9 The Address Bar.

The **Address** bar is the main way of opening new Web pages when you know their URLs. A drop-down menu of the most recent locations you have entered, can be opened by tapping or clicking the arrowhead, the **Autocomplete** ▾ button, at the right of the address box.

Explorer Buttons

The **Internet Explorer** is fully equipped with toolbars, which have buttons you can tap or click to quickly carry out a program function, as shown below in Fig. 5.10.

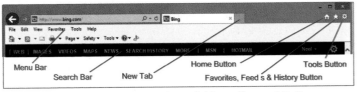

Fig. 5.10 The Internet Explorer Address Bar and Buttons.

It is possible to add several toolbars to the above display by touching and holding or right-clicking on an empty part on the top blue band of the above screen to display a drop-down menu of **Toolbar** options shown in Fig. 5.11 overleaf.

Explorer Toolbars

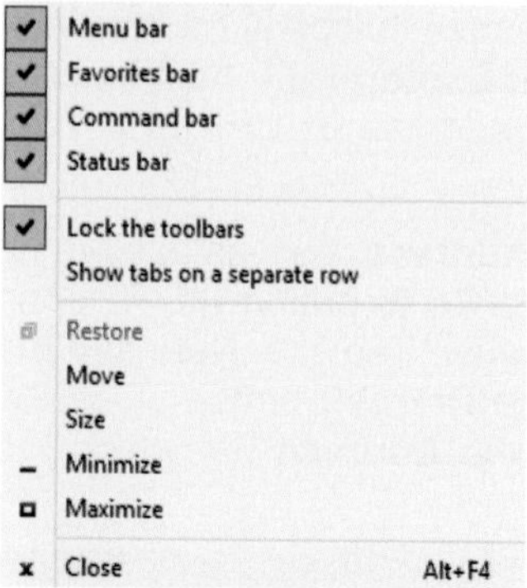

You can choose which toolbars to display by tapping or clicking the ones you want to see. This places a tick mark against the selected toolbar. Tapping or clicking again a selected toolbar, deselects it.

Fig. 5.12 shows what you'll see if all the toolbars on the list were to be selected.

Fig. 5.11 The Toolbars List.

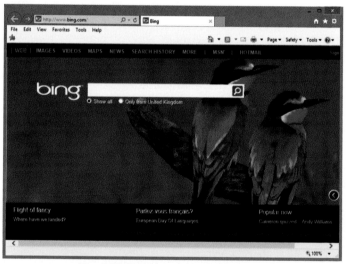

Fig. 5.12 Displaying All the Toolbars.

Tapping or clicking the down-arrowhead at the extreme right of the **Status** bar (at the bottom of Fig. 5.12), opens a menu of **Zoom** options, as shown here in Fig. 5.13.

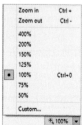

Fig. 5.13 Zoom Options.

Most of the buttons on the **Address** bar and other toolbars are pretty self-explanatory. Those on the **Address** bar have the following functions:

Button		*Function*
←	**Back**	Displays the previous page viewed. If there isn't one this is 'greyed out'.
→	**Forward**	Displays the next page on the **History** list.
▼	**Autocomplete**	Opens a drop-down menu of the autocomplete address bar pages.
🖼	**Compatibility**	Improves the display of Web sites designed for older browsers.
↻	**Refresh**	Brings a fresh copy of the current Web page to the viewer.
✕	**Stop**	Halts any on-line transfer of data.
🔍	**Search**	Searches for the text typed into the **Search** box.

Compatibility Mode

You may find that **Internet Explorer 10** does not render some older Web pages correctly. One of my online banking sites for example has some problems with pagination. To resolve these types of problem, just tap or click the **Compatibility View** 🖼 button at the right end of the **Address** bar. This displays the Web site as it would be if viewed in a previous version of **Internet Explorer**, and usually corrects display problems like misaligned text, images, or text boxes.

This only affects the Web site that was active when you select the **Compatibility View** button, other sites open at the same time will still use normal **Explorer** functionality.

The **Compatibility View** 🖼 button only seems to appear on the **Address** bar when it may be needed, so as time goes by and Web developers bring their sites up to 'scratch' you probably won't see it very often!

The Menu Bar

The **Menu** bar is located below the **Address** bar (see Fig. 5.12). It displays sub-menus when one of its menu options (**File**, **Edit**, **View**, **Favorites**, **Tools** or **Help**) is selected. Fig. 5.14 shows the sub-menu of **Help** and what displays if you select the **About Internet Explorer** option.

Fig. 5.14 The Internet Options Dialogue Box.

Most of the **Menu** bar options are fairly self-explanatory, so I leave you to investigate them by yourself. The only option that merits deliberation in some detail is **Favorites**, to be discussed shortly.

The Command Bar

The **Command** bar, below the **Menu** toolbar (see Fig. 5.14), has the following default buttons:

Button	Function
🏠 **Home**	Displays your specified home page, with a Microsoft page as the default.
📶 **Feeds**	View Feeds on the open Web site. If a feed is not detected the colour of the icon remains grey.
✉ **Read Mail**	Opens your mail client so that you can read your e-mail messages.

	Print	Prints the open Web page, or frame, using the current print settings.
Page ▾		Opens a menu that allows you to open a new window, save the current page, send it or a link to send it by e-mail to a recipient, zoom the page, or change the text size on it.
Safety ▾		Displays a drop-down menu that allows you to delete the browsing **History**, browse in private, see the privacy policy of Web pages, turn on the **SmartScreen Filter** so that unsafe Web sites can be reported, and activate **Windows Update**.
Tools ▾		Displays a drop-down menu that allows you to diagnose connection problems, reopen the last browsing session, manage pop-ups, specify your Internet options, and generally control how **Explorer** works.
	Help	Opens a drop-down menu giving quick access to **Help** topics.

The Favorites Bar

The **Favorites** bar has the following buttons:

Button	*Function*
Favorites	Opens the **Favorites Center** from which you can choose the **Favorites**, **Feeds** or **History** bars.
Add to	Adds a favourite site to the **Favorites** bar.

In addition, there are links to suggested Microsoft Web sites.

Favorites

Using **Favorites** (Bookmarks), is an easy way to save Web page addresses for future use. It's much easier to select a

page from a sorted list, than to manually type a URL address into the **Address** field. You don't have to remember the address and are less likely to make a typing error!

With **Internet Explorer** your **Favorites** are kept in the **Favorites Center**, shown in Fig. 5.15, opened by clicking the button.

Fig. 5.15 Favorites.

To keep the list open in a separate pane, you click the **Pin the Favorites Center** button. To close it again, click its **Close** button.

Adding a Favorite – There are several ways to add a **Favorite** to your list:

One way is to click the **Add to Favorites** button to add the address of the Web page you are viewing to a **Favorites** bar which displays to the right of the **Add to Favorites** button. Another way is to touch and hold or right-click the Web page you are viewing and select **Add to Favorites** from the drop-down menu. This opens the **Add a Favorite** dialogue box (Fig. 5.16) in which you can give the new **Favorite** a name, and choose a folder to put it in. Then just tap or click the **Add** button to finish.

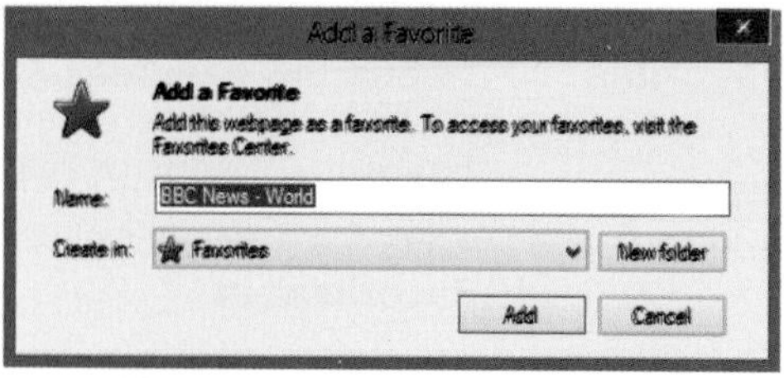

Fig. 5.16 The Add a Favorite Box.

Browsing History

Internet Explorer stores details of all the Web pages and files you view on your hard disc, and places temporary pointers to them in a folder. To return to these in the future, tap or click the **View History** tab in the **Favorites Center**, to open the **History** list shown in Fig. 5.17.

Fig. 5.17 Web Browsing History.

In this list you can see what Web sites you visited in the last 3 weeks. Tapping or clicking a listed site opens links to the individual Web pages you went to. Selecting any of these will open the page again.

The length of time history items are kept on your hard disc can be set by using the **Tools** button and selecting **Internet Options** to open the tabbed dialogue box shown in Fig. 5.18.

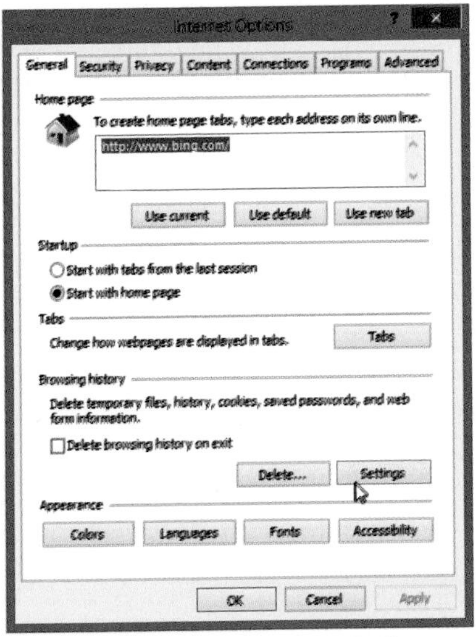

Tapping or clicking the **Settings** button in the **Browsing history** section, pointed to here, opens an additional dialogue box in which you can select the number of days that **History** files are kept (between 0 and 999) in the **History** tab. To delete all history items click the **Delete** button in the **Internet Options** box, which will release the hard disc space used.

Fig. 5.18 General Internet Options.

Web Feeds

Web feeds (feeds for short) are usually used for news and blogs and contain frequently updated content published by a Web site. You can use feeds if you want updates to a Web site to be automatically downloaded to your PC.

When you visit a Web page that contains feeds, the grey **Feeds** button on the Internet Explorer toolbar changes to orange. To look at the feeds, click the feed symbol. To get content automatically downloaded to your computer, you will need to subscribe to the feed. This is very easy to do, and doesn't cost anything! Just tapping or clicking a **Subscribe to this feed** link, like that shown in Fig. 5.19, opens the **Subscribe to this Feed** box shown in Fig. 5.20.

BBC News - UK

You are viewing a feed that contains frequently updated content. When you subscribe to a feed, it is added to the Common Feed List. Updated information from the feed is automatically downloaded to your computer and can be viewed in Internet Explorer and other programs. Learn more about feeds.

Subscribe to this feed

Fig. 5.19 Subscribing to a Web Feed.

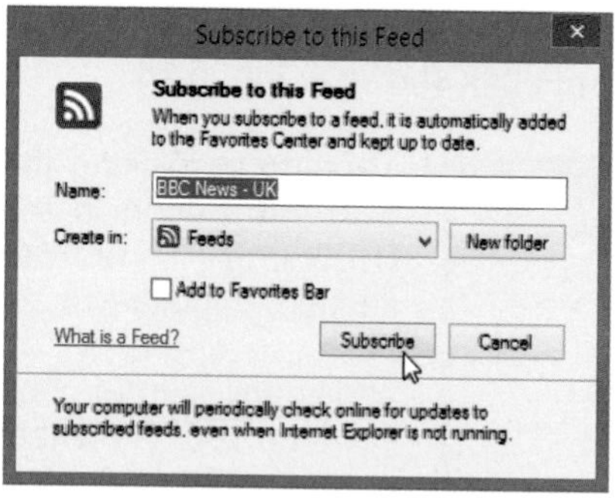

Clicking the **Subscribe** button adds the feed to the 'Common Feed List' in the **Favorites Center**, and updated information from the feed will be automatically down-loaded to your computer for viewing in **Internet Explorer**.

Fig. 5.20 Subscribe to this Feed Box.

All your subscribed feeds will be listed in the **Feeds** section of the **Favorites Center**. Selecting an item in the **Feeds** list, shown in Fig. 5.21, will open it in the main **Explorer** pane so you can keep up to date.

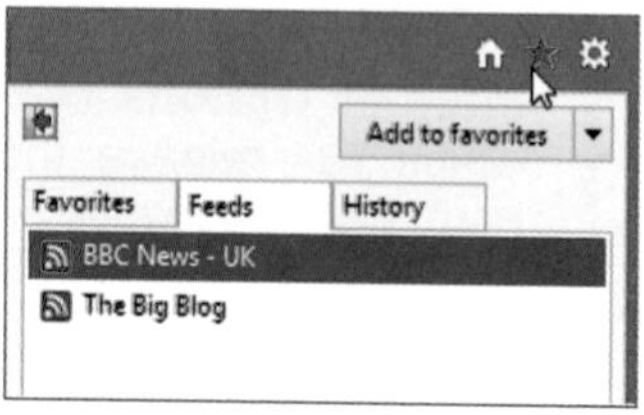

Fig. 5.21 Feeds List.

Tabbed Browsing

With tabbed browsing you can open several Web sites in one **Explorer** window each in its own tab, and switch between them by clicking on their tab. To create a new tab, tap or click the **New Tab** icon ▣, pointed to in Fig. 5.22, immediately to the right of the existing tabs.

Fig. 5.22 Creating a New Tab.

Selecting the **New Tab** icon, displays the same address in the **Address** bar which you'll have to replace with a new address.

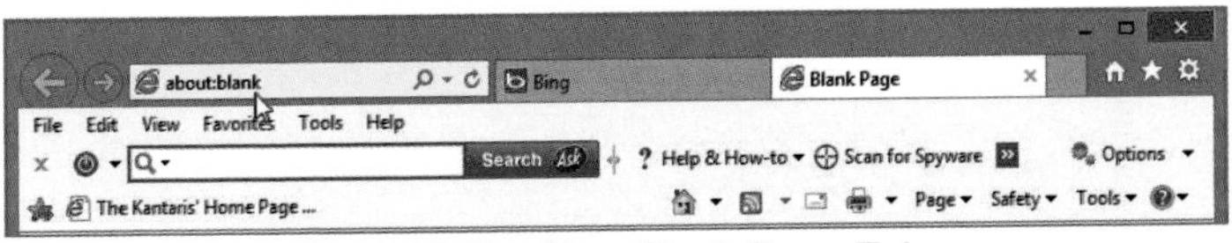

Fig. 5.23 The New Blank Page Tab.

Next, tap or click the entry in the **Address** bar to select it, then simply type a new Web address, or use the **Favorites** button ▣ or select **Favorites** from the **Menu** bar and open one of your **Favorites**.

Explorer 10 has an **InPrivate Browsing** mode opened by selecting **Tools** in the **Menu** bar, as shown in Fig. 5.24. This opens a new window with information about the **InPrivate** mode and also informs you that it has been turned on. You can now safely browse without leaving any traces. Just closing the **InPrivate** window returns you to standard mode.

Fig. 5.24 The Tools Menu Bar Options.

Saving and Opening a Group of Tabs

To save a group of tabs so that you can open the pages again, do the following: Open the Web sites you want to save, maybe ones with a common theme. Tap or click the **Favorites** ⭐ button to open the **Favorites Center**, then click the down-arrow by the **Add to Favorites** ⭐ button, and select **Add Current Tabs to Favorites** from the drop-down list.

In the displayed dialogue box give a name to the folder to contain the selected Web sites – I called it **Best Buys**, (Fig. 5.25) and click the **Add** button.

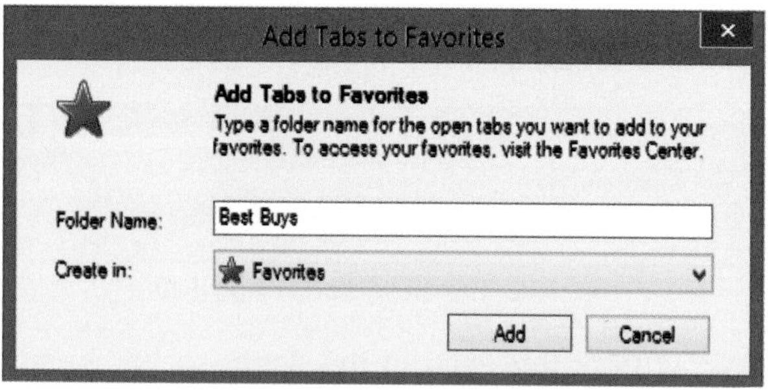

Fig. 5.25 The Add Tabs to Favorites Box.

To open a group of tabs, click the **Favorites** ⭐ button, select the group folder you want to open (see Fig. 5.26), and either click the arrow to the right of the folder name ➡ to open all the tabbed sites in the group, or tap/click the folder to display all the Web sites in it and select one of them.

Fig. 5.26 Opening a Group of Tabs.

Changing your Search Engine

You could change which Internet search engine you are using, if you are not happy with **bing**. For example, to change to **Google**, type **www.google.co.uk** in the **Address** bar (see Fig. 5.27) and either press the **Enter** key on the keyboard or tap/click the **Go to** → button to the right of the **Address** bar to open **Google**'s UK search page, as shown in Fig. 5.27.

Fig. 5.27 The Google Internet Browser.

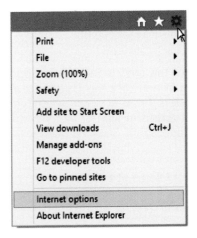

Fig. 5.28 The Tools Menu.

To make **Google** your default search engine, click the **Tools** ⚙ icon (also pointed to at the top-right corner in Fig. 5.28), to open the **Tools** menu shown here in Fig. 5.28. From here click the **Internet options** entry to open the multi-tab dialogue box shown in Fig. 5.29 on the next page.

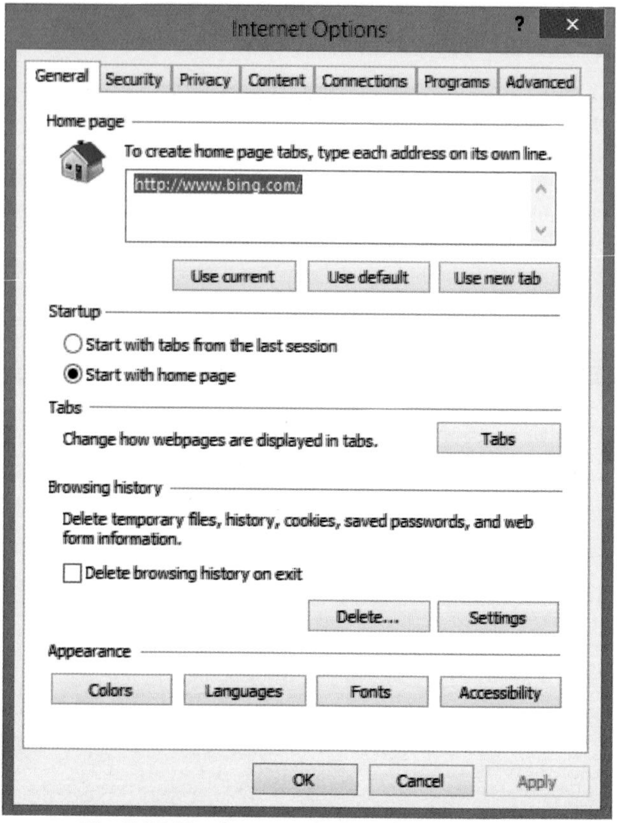

Fig. 5.29 The Internet Options Dialogue Box.

All you have to do now is replace the entry in the **Home page** text box with **www.google.co.uk/** and click the **Use current** button, followed by the **OK** button. From now on, whenever you tap or click on the **Internet Explorer** icon or tile, you will be displaying the **Google** UK page.

Note: As this book is about Microsoft's Windows 8, I'll continue with what is supplied with it. Therefore, in what follows the **bing** search engine will be used.

Getting Help

You can get help with **Internet Explorer** as well as with **bing**.

Internet Explorer Help

You can get help with **Explorer** by tapping or clicking the **Help** 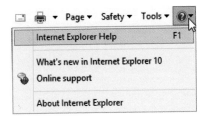 button at the extreme right of the **Toolbar** and selecting the **Internet Explorer Help** entry from the drop-down menu of options shown in Fig. 5.30.

Fig. 5.30 Getting Help with Internet Explorer.

This displays the **Internet Explorer Help** screen shown in Fig. 5.31 below.

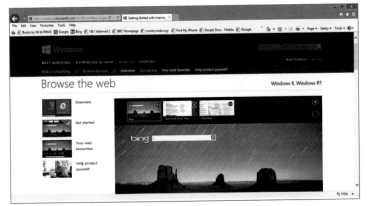

Fig. 5.31 The Internet Explorer Help Screen.

You can work your way through the items listed on the left of the screen at your leisure. What is displayed first is the **Get Started** option.

Getting Help with Bing

You can get help with **bing** by activating the **Help** entry at the bottom of a **bing** screen, highlighted in Fig. 5.32 below.

Fig. 5.32 The Bing Help Link.

This opens the **BING HELP** screen shown in Fig. 5.33 below which lists several help topics and the ability to search for a particular topic.

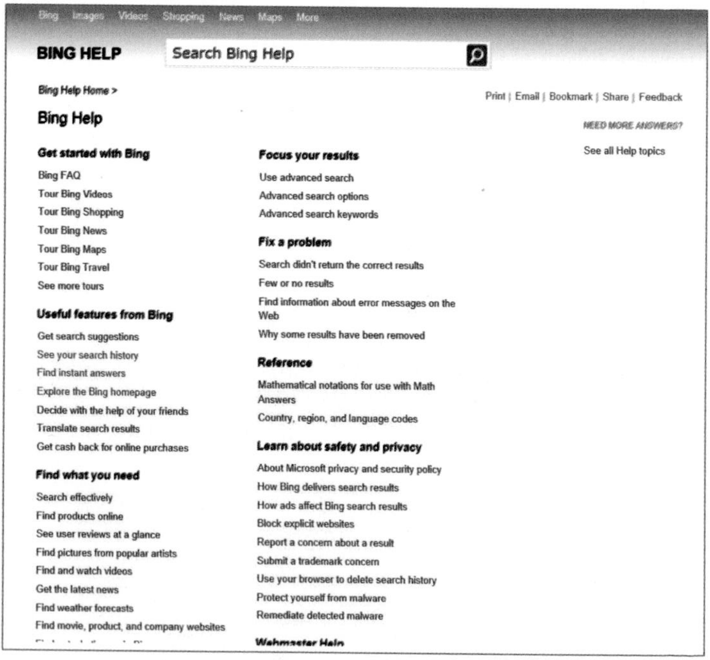

Fig. 5.33 The Bing Help Topics Screen.

Perhaps you can get back to this page when you need help with some topic. In the mean time you might like to take a **Tour** from the comprehensive list available under **Get started with bing.**

6

Keeping in Touch

The E-mail App

Windows 8 comes with a **Mail** App, the tile of which is to be found at the top-left corner of the **Start** screen. It is a similar program to the one in Windows **Live Essentials**. The App is designed to work with Windows 8 and as long as you are connected to the Internet and set up correctly, you can communicate with others by e-mail wherever they are in the world, all you need to know is their e-mail address. In this chapter I look at Windows Mail, but you can also use another program if you prefer.

Connecting to Your Server

If you already have a **Live** mail account, then the **Mail** App will detect it, if not, then when you start **Mail** for the first time, you will be prompted to add one. You will need the following information from the supplier of your e-mail service:

- Your e-mail address and password

- The type of e-mail server to be used

- The address of the incoming and outgoing e-mail servers you should use.

If the connection process does not start automatically, use the **Settings** charm, pointed to in Fig. 6.1, to display the **Settings** screen, the top-half of which is shown in Fig. 6.2 on the next page.

Fig. 6.1 The Settings Charm.

Fig. 6.2 The
Settings Menu.

Next, select the **Accounts** option pointed to in Fig. 6.2, to display Fig. 6.3. Activating the **Add an account** option, displays the screen shown in Fig. 6.4.

Fig. 6.3 Adding
an Account.

Fig. 6.4 The Add an
Account Options.

As you can see in Fig. 6.4, you have a number of choices of Internet-based accounts, but if you have an Internet-based account that is not listed or you need to add an account based on a Website, then you can choose the **Other Account** option.

You can add all your different e-mail accounts by following the same procedure so you can view them all from the same window. Once your connection is established, opening the **Inbox** will display any messages waiting in your mailbox, as shown in Fig. 6.5 on the next page.

This shows the default layout of the Windows **Mail** screen, which consists of the **Folder Pane** on the left, a **Message List** in the centre and a **Reading Pane** on the right with a Message header above it.

The **Folder Pane** contains the active mail folders, such as **Inbox**, **Drafts**, **Sent items**, **Outbox**, **Junk** and **Deleted items**. Tapping or clicking one of these, displays its contents in the **Message List**. Selecting a message in the list, opens a preview of it in the **Reading Pane**.

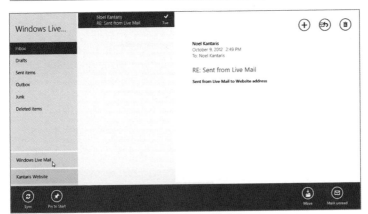

Fig. 6.5 The Windows Mail Screen.

To check your mail at any time, either swipe upwards from the bottom of the screen or right-click the mouse to display the dark blue band shown in the composite above which allows you to access the tools shown on it. Activating the **Sync** button will automatically download your messages, if you have a Broadband connection.

A Test E-mail Message

Before explaining in more detail other features of Windows **Mail**, I will step through the procedure of sending a very simple e-mail message. The best way to test out any unfamiliar e-mail features is to send a test message to your own e-mail address. This saves wasting somebody else's time, and the message can be checked very quickly. In fact, this is what was done above.

To start, touch or click the **New** ⊕ button at the top-right corner of the screen shown in Fig. 6.5, to open the **New Message** window, shown in Fig. 6.6 on the next page.

Type your own e-mail address in the **To** field, and a title for the message in the **Add a subject** field which will form a header for the message when it is received, so it helps to show in a few words what the message is about.

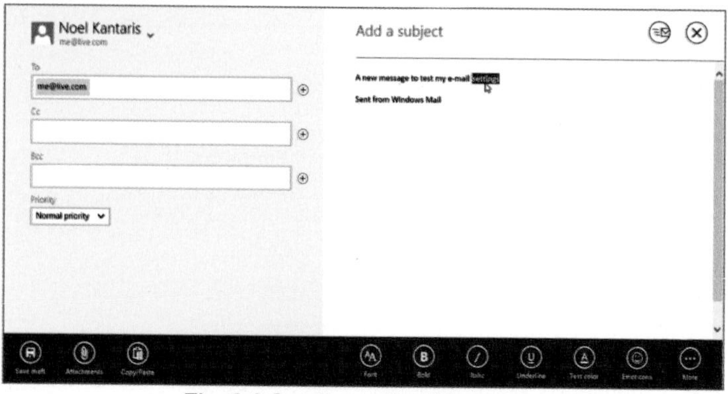

Fig. 6.6 Sending a Test Message.

Next, type your own text in the **Add a message** field as shown above. Note that the moment a word (or several words) are highlighted in the main message, a bar of tools displays at the bottom of the screen which allow you to enhance your text, change its colour, increase its font size, add emoticons and much more. Finally, if you make mistakes and want to delete the message, press the **Delete** ⊗ button otherwise press the **Send** 🖃 button.

By default, your message is placed in the **Outbox** folder and sent immediately if you are on Broadband. When **Mail** next checks for mail, it should find the message and download it into your **Inbox** folder.

Note: The **Bcc** field and **Priority** shown in Fig. 6.6 only display when you activate the **Show more** option which is usually to be found just below the **Cc** field.

Cc in Fig. 6.6 stands for 'carbon copy'. Anyone listed in the **Cc** field of a message receives a copy of that message when you send it. All other recipients of that message can see that the person you designated as a **Cc** recipient received a copy of the message.

Bcc stands for 'blind carbon copy'. **Bcc** recipients are invisible to all the other recipients of the message (including other **Bcc** recipients).

Activating the down arrow against the **Priority** field, displays the available options as shown in Fig. 6.7. You can change the priority if you need to, but the default is normally good enough.

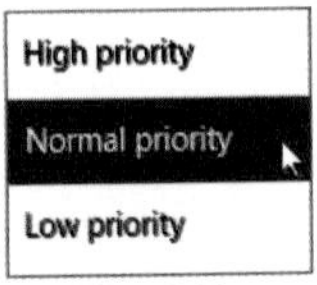

Fig. 6.7.

Replying to a Message

When you receive an e-mail message that you want to reply to, **Mail** makes it very easy to do. The reply address and the new message subject fields are both added automatically for you. Also, by default, the original message is quoted in the reply window for you to edit as required.

With the message you want to reply to still open, tap or click the **Respond** ⊕ button to display the available options, shown in Fig. 6.8. As you can see, you can **Reply** only to the person who sent you the message, or to all the people who received the message. The **Forward** option is used to forward the message to another person altogether, in which case you'll have to supply their e-mail address.

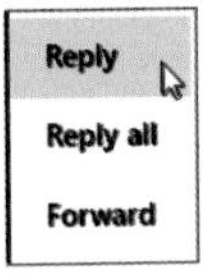

Fig. 6.8.

Using E-mail Attachments

To add an attachment to an e-mail message, such as a photo or work file, simply tap or click the **Attach** 📎 button to be found in the bar of tools when you either highlight a word, swipe from the bottom of the screen upwards or right-click the mouse button. Doing so displays what is shown here.

Fig. 6.9 Selecting Files.

You can now browse your computer to find the item you want to attach, including your libraries where you might have saved documents or pictures. Below, selected photos in my pictures library are shown in the process of being attached.

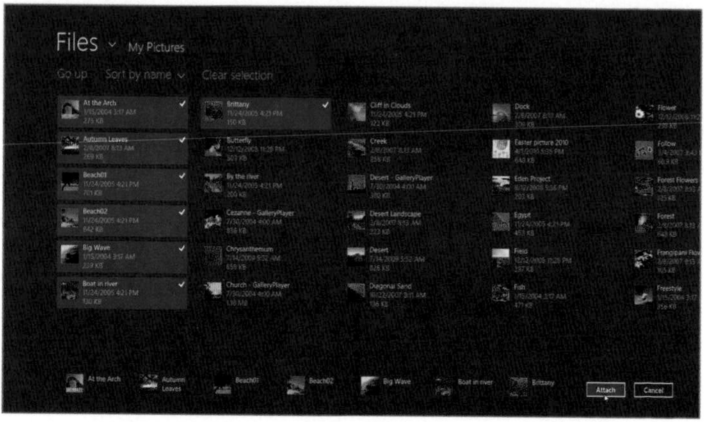

Fig. 6.10 Selecting Photos to Attach to a Message.

Having selected the photos you want to attach, tap or click the **Attach** button to complete the process. Your e-mail should now look similar to the one shown in Fig. 6.11.

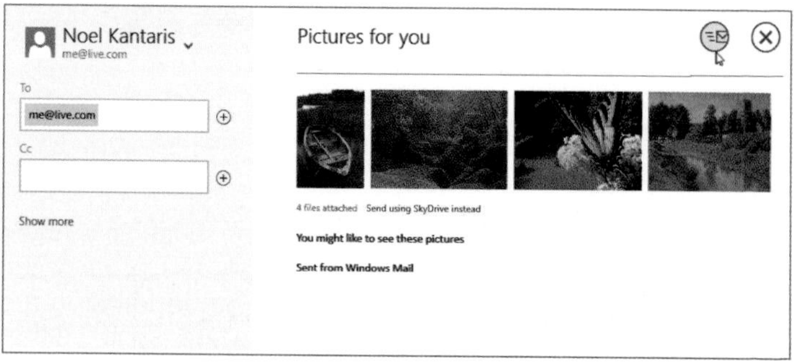

Fig. 6.11 An E-mail Message with Attached Photos.

All you have to do now is send the e-mail, perhaps to yourself, so you can see and check the result. In the screen above you are also invited to send your pictures via **SkyDrive** instead. More about this later.

Receiving Attachments

Fig. 6.12 below, shows the e-mail you'll receive with its attachments had you sent it to yourself.

Fig. 6.12 Received E-mail Message with Attached Photos.

The received message shows the (**.jpg**) pictures together with their name (if already named) and size and you are invited to download them. Having done so, you can tap or click each picture in turn to open the **Options** menu as shown in Fig. 6.13.

Fig. 6.13 Options to Open or Save Received Photos.

If you choose to **Open**, the picture will be displayed full screen. You also have the choice to **Open with** a particular program capable of editing the picture. Selecting **Save**, a screen similar to that shown in Fig. 6.10 is displayed from where you can choose to **Go up** should you want to choose a place to save the attachment other that your **Pictures** library.

Obviously, trying to save a document rather than a picture, **Mail** will attempt to save it to the **Document** library.

Deleting Messages

Some e-mail messages you receive will be worth keeping, but most will need deleting. From the **Read Message** window you just tap or click the **Delete** ⊚ button to do this.

Whenever you delete a message it is actually moved to the **Deleted items** folder. If ignored, this folder gets bigger and bigger over time, so you need to check it frequently and manually re-delete messages you will not need again.

Sending an E-mail to the Drafts Folder

If you decide that your e-mail is not complete yet and further changes are needed before sending it, use the **Save Draft** ⊟ button to be found on the bar of tools at the bottom of the screen when you swipe the edge from the bottom of the screen upwards or right-click the mouse button.

To complete the process, close the e-mail down by activating the **Close** ⊗ button and selecting to **Save draft** from the displayed menu option.

This allows you to retrieve later the e-mail from the **Drafts** folder for further editing prior to sending it off.

Summary of System Folders

Windows **Mail** has six folders which it always keeps intact and will not let you delete. Most of these have been discussed already, but here is a summary of their function.

- The **Inbox** folder holds all incoming messages. Messages in the **Inbox** folder can be moved or copied into any other folder except the **Outbox** folder.

- The **Outbox** folder holds messages that have been prepared but not yet transmitted. As soon as the messages are sent they are automatically removed to the **Sent items** folder.

- The **Sent items** folder holds messages that have been transmitted. You can then decide whether to 'file' copies of these messages, or whether to delete them. Messages in the **Sent items** folder can be moved or copied into any of the other folders except the **Outbox** folder.

- The **Deleted items** folder holds messages that have been deleted and placed in there as a safety feature. Messages in the **Deleted items** folder can be moved or copied into any of the other folders, except the **Outbox** folder.

- The **Drafts** folder is used to hold a message you closed down without sending by selecting the **Save Draft** toolbar button, then the menu option when you try to close it. Messages in the **Drafts** folder cannot be moved or copied into any of the other folders. Simply tap or click such a message to open it, edit it, and then send it.

- The **Junk** folder (also referred to as **Spam** by some e-mail accounts) is designed to catch unsolicited e-mail messages.

Printing Messages

Occasionally you might receive an important e-mail message that you would like to print and file for safe keeping. This is easy with Windows 8, once you are shown how to do it.

First, display the e-mail you want to print on your computer's screen, then activate the **Charms** bar and tap or click **Devices** which opens its window and displays the printers available to you, as shown in Fig. 6.14 on the next page. Your screen will most certainly look different, but it is assumed here that the printer you want to use is connected to your computer and switched on. It is also assumed that what you display on your screen is the actual e-mail message, not a screen in **Internet Explorer** associated with the e-mail.

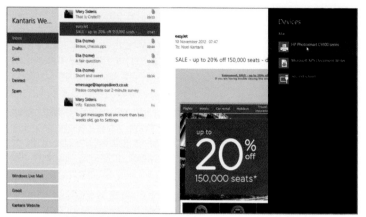

Fig. 6.14 The Message and Devices Options.

All you have to do to print the e-mail message is to tap or click on the printer of your choice to display a screen similar to that in Fig. 6.15. Tapping or clicking on the **Print** button starts the process.

Fig. 6.15 The Printer Options.

The People App

Windows **Mail** lets you create and keep a list of **People** (called 'contacts' in previous versions of Windows) to store details such as the names, addresses, phone numbers, and e-mail addresses of all those you communicate with most.

If you have upgraded to Windows 8, your 'contacts' would have automatically been transferred across, but if you have installed Windows 8 onto a partition, then your **People** list will contain only the contacts you have added or imported into the program from mail accounts you add to Windows **Mail**. If you add **Live Mail** or **Gmail** into Windows **Mail**, then the 'contacts' list associated with these services will be tansported across.

If all is well, selecting the **People** App on the **Start** screen, should change your screen to one similar to that in Fig. 6.16.

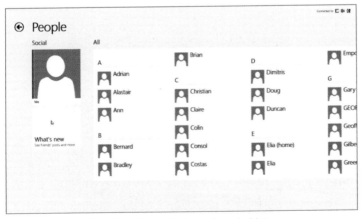

Fig. 6.16 The Windows People List.

In Fig. 6.16, only a small part of the **People** App's content, is shown, but to preserve anonymity, all surnames have been removed from the above screen.

You can add a new person's details by first swiping upwards from the bottom of the screen (or right-clicking with the mouse) to reveal the **Tools** bar at the bottom of the screen, then selecting the **Add** ⊕ button to display the screen shown in Fig. 6.17 below.

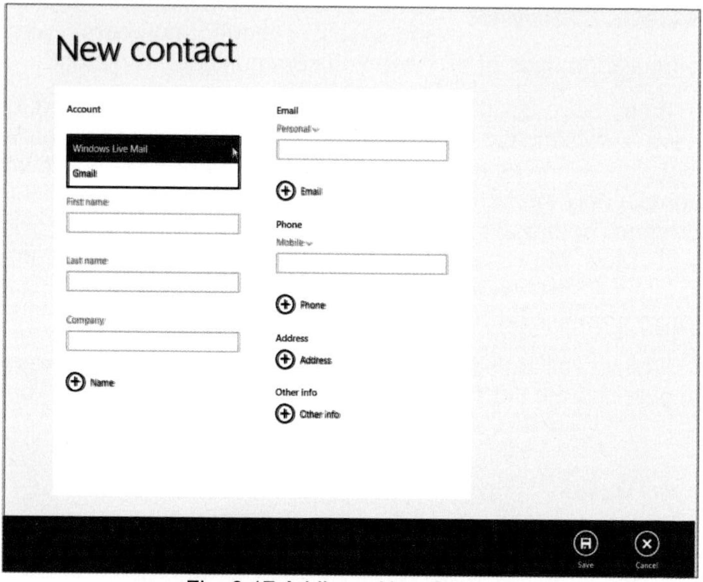

Fig. 6.17 Adding a New Contact.

You can select either account from the drop down menu; **Live Mail** or **Gmail**, because the information will be synchronised and it will display in the **People** App's content. You can now enter the name, phone, and e-mail details for your new contact. Personal information can be entered if you have the time, or entered later by editing the contact's entry.

To edit or delete a contact, tap it or double-click it to open it in its own screen, then swipe upwards or right-click to reveal the **Tools** bar at the bottom of the screen and select either the **Edit** ⊘ button or the **Delete** ⊙ button.

Unfortunately, there does not seem to be any facility for adding photos of your contacts, as in earlier versions.

To send a new message from your **People** list, open their entry in the **People** list, as shown in Fig. 6.18, and tap or click the **Send email** button to open a pre-addressed **New Message** window in **Mail**.

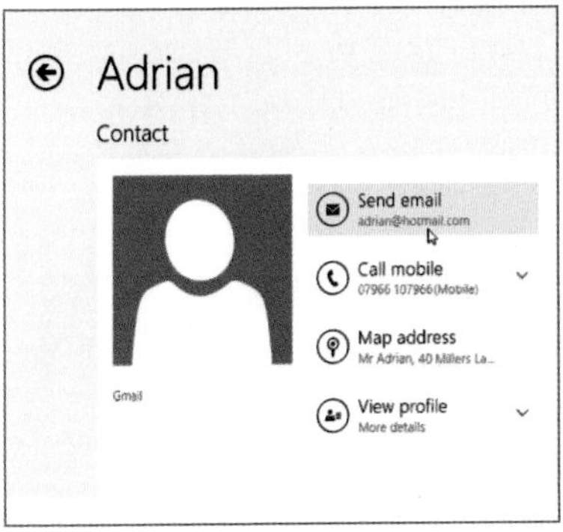

One rather nice touch here is that, if you have entered an address for a person, tapping or clicking the **Map address** button, opens up a map showing the person's address, as shown in Fig. 6.19 below.

Fig. 6.18 Selecting a Mail Recipient.

Fig. 6.19 A Contact's Address on a Map.

The screen above is shown in the **Maps** App, which will be discussed in detail in Chapter 9.

The Messaging App

Another way of keeping in touch is through the **Messaging** App. Tapping or clicking its tile on the **Start** screen, opens the screen shown in Fig. 6.20.

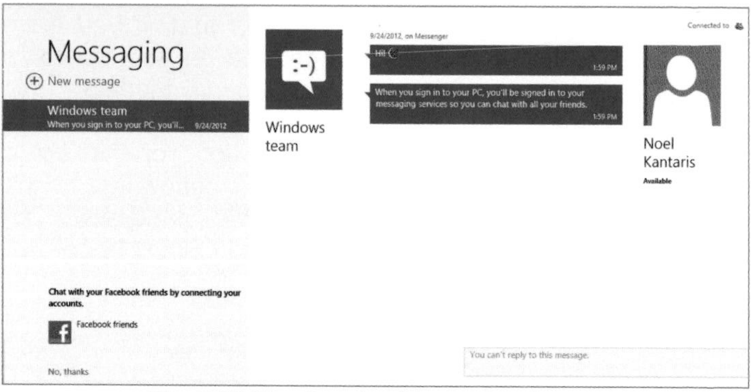

Fig. 6.20 The Opening Messaging Screen.

There is a welcoming message from the Windows team letting know what you can do with **Messaging**. For example, you can tap or click the **Facebook** icon to log on to your account and chat with your friends.

Fig. 6.21 The Opening Messaging Screen Showing Facebook.

The Calendar App

The Windows 8 **Start** screen also provides you with a **Calendar** tile which when you tap or click, opens the screen shown in Fig. 6.22.

Fig. 6.22 The Live Mail Calendar.

Above, an entry was tapped or clicked to display the message **This is a recurring event** and underneath **Open one** or **Open series**. As a recurring event, there is obviously a series of repeated events which you can choose to open so that you can edit the entry, as shown in Fig. 6.23.

Details			Remembrance Day
When			Add a message
November ∨	11 Sunday ∨	2012 ∨	
Start			
12 ∨	00 ∨	AM ∨	
How long			
All day ∨			
Where			
Calendar			
■ me@gmail.com			
Show more			

Fig. 6.23
Opening a
Calendar
Entry to Edit.

Similarly, you can make a new entry in your calendar, by tapping or clicking on a given day to display the screen below. Here, the **Show more** link in Fig. 6.23 has been activated, so more information is displayed, as shown in Fig. 6.24

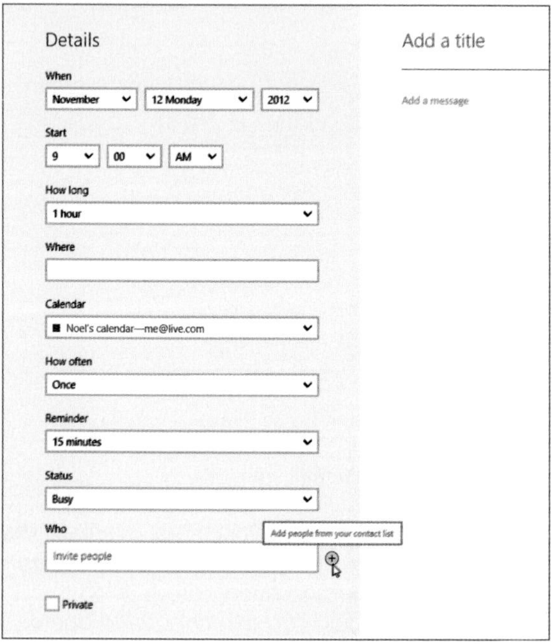

Details   Add a title

When
| November ⌄ | 12 Monday ⌄ | 2012 ⌄ | Add a message

Start
| 9 ⌄ | 00 ⌄ | AM ⌄ |

How long
| 1 hour   ⌄ |

Where
| |

Calendar
| ■ Noel's calendar—me@live.com   ⌄ |

How often
| Once   ⌄ |

Reminder
| 15 minutes   ⌄ |

Status
| Busy   ⌄ |

Who   Add people from your contact list
| invite people   ⊕ |

☐ Private

Fig. 6.24
Entering a
New
Calendar
Entry.

This provides you with all the scheduling tools you will ever need. You can enter appointments, birthdays, or fix meetings with other people and invite them to the meeting. It also supports day, week and month views (see Fig. 6.25) and you can have multiple, colour-coded calendars, making it easy to keep schedules for work, family, school and hobbies, etc.

Fig. 6.25 The Toolbar of the Main Calendar Screen.

It is worth spending sometime exploring this excellent facility.

7

The SkyDrive Facility

Microsoft's **SkyDrive** is one of the best Web storage services available. You get 7 GB free Web space to store you photos and documents so you can access them from wherever you happen to be. You can also invite other users to access your files for sharing or editing shared documents.

> **Note:** SkyDrive should be treated as a means of sharing and accessing files when away from your computer, not as a secure place to store your only copies of photos or other work!

SkyDrive is pre-installed on Windows 8 and has its own tile on the **Start** menu, shown here. Tapping or clicking this tile opens a screen similar to that in Fig. 7.1.

Fig. 7.1 The Initial SkyDrive Screen with Toolbar Active.

In this case, **SkyDrive** shows some of the default folders empty. To display the toolbar at the bottom of the screen, as shown in Fig. 7.1, with relevant tool buttons to the work being carried out at the time, either swipe upwards from the bottom of the screen or click the right mouse button.

Creating a Folder on SkyDrive

You can create additional folders or sub-folders by tapping or clicking the **New Folder** button, which displays the box shown in Fig. 7.2, where a name can be given for a new folder and created by tapping or clicking the **Create folder** button. Once this is done, open the newly created folder, as shown in Fig. 7.3

Fig. 7.2 Creating a New Folder.

below, then use the **Upload** button to save files into it either as an additional backup or because you might want to access these files when away from home.

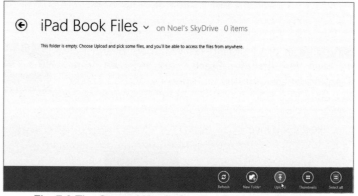

Fig. 7.3 The Opened Newly Created Folder on SkyDrive.

It is important to open the folder into which you want to upload the files, otherwise they might be uploaded to a different folder! Once you activate the **Upload** button, Windows allows you access to the files on your computer so you can select the files you want by tapping or clicking them, then using the **Add to SkyDrive** button (it only appears on the toolbar after you start selecting files) to begin the process of uploading, as shown in Fig. 7.4 on the next page.

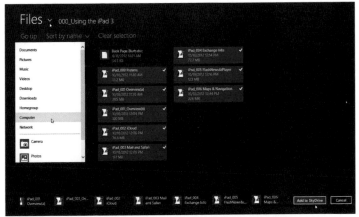

Fig. 7.4 Selecting Required Files to Upload.

Tapping or clicking the down arrow next to **Files**, pointed to at the top of the screen in Fig. 7.4, displays a list of possible places on your hard drive for you to choose from. Selecting **Computer**, allows you to get to files on your hard disc which, in this example, were chosen specifically because they were very large in size, ranging from 13.2 to 226 MB. As you tap or click on such files, a tick mark appears next to their entry and a thumbnail is added at the bottom of the screen. Activating the **Add to SkyDrive** button at the bottom of the screen, also pointed to in Fig. 7.4, starts the uploading process.

The time taken to upload files depends on the speed of your Broadband connection and the size and number of files selected, so be patient as it could take some time!

> **Note:** Also be aware that there is a limit to the maximum size of a file that you are allowed to upload. If your files are larger than 100 MB (this might increase later), it is advisable that you either split them, Zip them or turn them into a PDF type before uploading.

Files larger than 100 MB will not upload, but produce an error as discussed next.

In fact, I had to experiment to find out the maximum size of file that would upload, with the result shown in Fig. 7.5 below.

Fig. 7.5 The Upload and Rejected Files.

The result of the experiment showed all files below 100 MB in size uploaded correctly, but all files above 100 MB were rejected. It was necessary to experiment, because information on the Internet persistently gave the maximum allowable file size as 50 MB which clearly is not the case.

Using the Shared Folder

The **Shared** folder on **SkyDrive** is used for sharing photos and other document files with friends or family. To start, go to **SkyDrive**, then:

- Tap or click the **Shared** folder to open it.

- Swipe upwards from the bottom edge of the screen or right-click to open the **Tools** bar.

- Tap or click the **Upload** 🔼 button.

- If you want to upload photos, select **Pictures** (refer to Fig. 7.4) which allows you to get to your photos on your hard disc.

- Select the photos you want to share, then tap or click the **Add to SkyDrive** button at the bottom of the screen.

The selected pictures are uploaded into the **Shared** folder.

Fig. 7.6 below, shows the contents of the **Shared** folder on my **SkyDrive**.

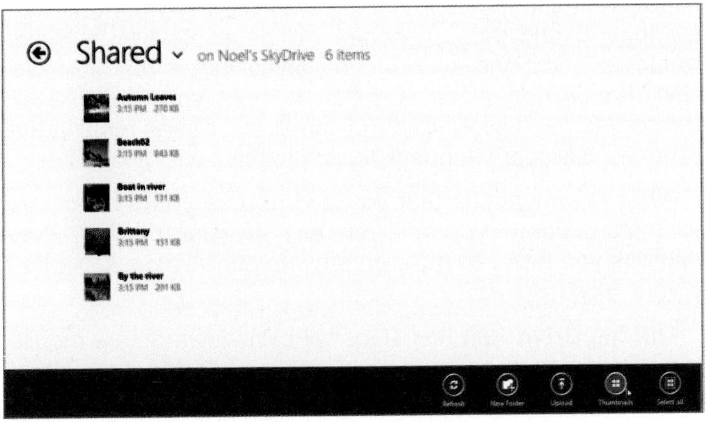

Fig. 7.6 The Contents of Shared Folder on SkyDrive.

Tapping or clicking the **Thumbnails** button, changes the display to that in Fig. 7.7.

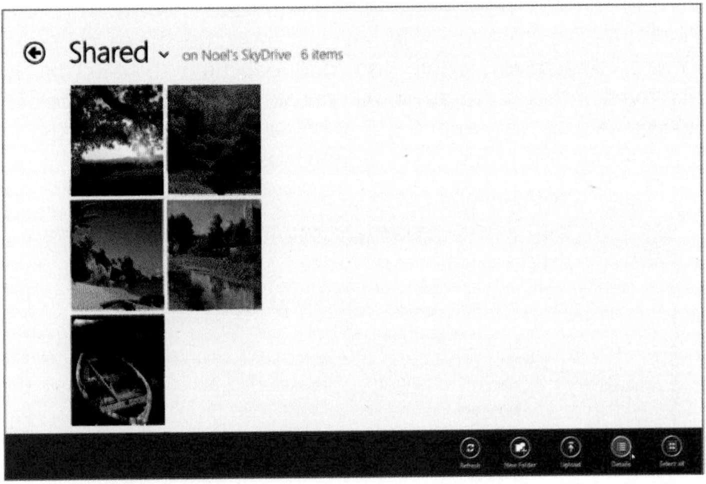

Fig. 7.7 The Contents of Shared Folder Displayed as Thumbnails.

You can now return to the display of Fig. 7.6 by tapping or clicking the **Details** button once more.

SkyDrive App and Desktop Application

Microsoft has changed and integrated **SkyDrive** for use with Windows 8 and these changes will be applied to users of Windows 7 and Vista. The idea behind this is that you use **SkyDrive** as the place in which to hold your documents, photos, etc., and allow your PC, tablet and phone running the Windows 8 Modern interface to synchronise with **SkyDrive**.

What this means is that you can access your documents no matter where you are, on any of your devices. Any changes you make to a file on any of your devices is applied to your **SkyDrive** file.

The **SkyDrive** App that ships with Windows 8, is a mobile App which you can use to view and change the contents of **SkyDrive**, but only if you are connected to the Internet. In other words, it only provides a live view of the contents of **SkyDrive**. If you are not connected to the Internet, you cannot see the contents of your **SkyDrive**.

In contrast, the desktop **SkyDrive** for Windows 8, allows you to create new files, edit them, etc., while you are disconnected from the Internet, but replicate these changes to the **SkyDrive**, when you connect next time. This is achieved through the automatic creation of a **SkyDrive** folder on you PC, as shown in Fig. 7.8 below. If the **Desktop** App is not on your computer, you can download it for free from:

http://windows.microsoft.com/en-GB/skydrive/download

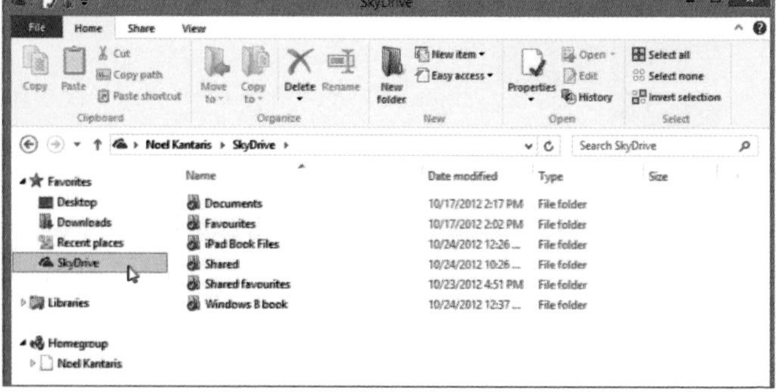

Fig. 7.8 The SkyDrive Folder on your PC.

Note: Since Windows RT does not allow the installation of external programs, the **Desktop** application for **SkyDrive**, cannot be download as described on the previous page.

Zipping Files

You can use the **Desktop** App of **SkyDrive** to zip files prior to uploading them to **SkyDrive**. You do this as follows:

- Start **File Explorer** and go to a place on your hard disc were you can select a large file to upload, as shown in the example in Fig. 7.9.

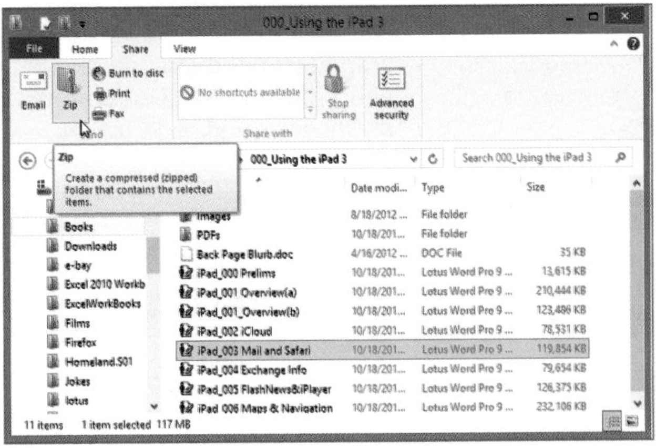

Fig. 7.9 Selecting Large Files on your PC.

- In the **Share** tab, activate the **Zip** option pointed to in Fig. 7.9 above.

- The selected file (which is almost 120 MB in size) will be zipped in a folder using the same name.

In Fig. 7.11 on the next page, you can see a drag and drop operation using the **File Explorer**. To be able to carry out this operation, you'll need to open two **File Explorer** windows as discussed next.

First, start **File Explorer** and locate **SkyDrive** on your **Folder List**, then open the **Documents** folder on your **SkyDrive**. Next, size the **Documents** window to something similar to that on the right of Fig. 7.11.

Fig. 7.10 The Right-click File Explorer Menu.

Now, touch and hold or right-click the **File Explorer** icon on the **Task** bar and select the **File Explorer**, pointed to on the displayed menu in Fig. 7.10. This is the only way to open two **File Explorer** windows on the screen at the same time. Next, size and move the newly opened window next to the **SkyDrive Documents** window and locate the file you want to upload on your hard disc. In this case, the zipped file has compressed to just over 20 MB. Finally, drag the zipped file from the left window and drop it in the **Documents** window, as shown in Fig. 7.11 below.

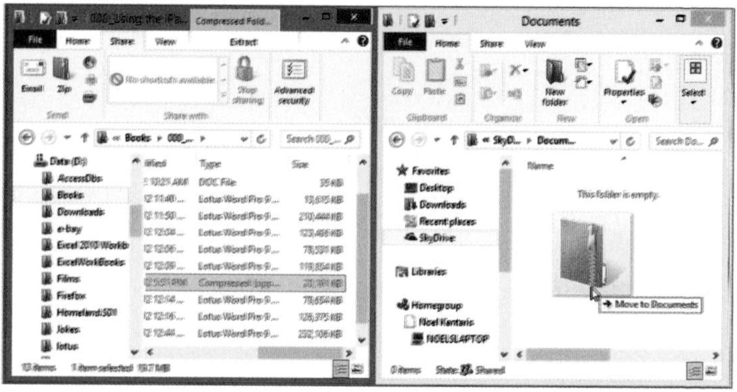

Fig. 7.11 Dragging and Dropping a Zipped File into the Documents Folder of SkyDrive.

Finally, revert to the Windows 8 mobile App to see the zipped file, as shown in Fig. 7.12 on the next page.

Fig. 7.12 The Zipped File on SkyDrive.

Tapping or clicking such a file opens it in the desktop version of **SkyDrive** from where you can retrieve the original file provided your PC has the program that created the original file installed.

A zipped file cannot be opened on the **SkyDrive** mobile App of Windows 8, so perhaps the moral of the story here is that you should avoid creating files larger that 100 MB, if you want to access them from mobile devices!

Uploading a PDF File

If you have a very large file and you want to be able to refer to it on a mobile device, but you haven't got to edit it, then perhaps the best solution is to convert the file to PDF format and upload that version.

For example, a book with a total size of 900 MB, can be reduced to just under 35 MB when converted to PDF format. That size file can then be uploaded using either the drag and drop desktop method described on the previous page, or the mobile **SkyDrive** App method described at the beginning of this chapter. The result is the same in the end, as shown in Fig. 7.13 on the next page.

Taping or clicking such a file opens it for you to examine, as shown on a mobile device in Fig. 7.14 also shown on the next page.

As you can see from the screen dump in Fig. 7.14, the mobile device in this case is an iPad (as seen at the top-left corner of the screen dump).

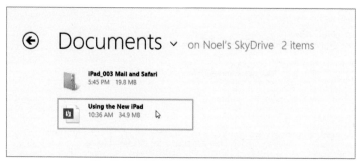

Fig. 7.13 The PDF File on SkyDrive.

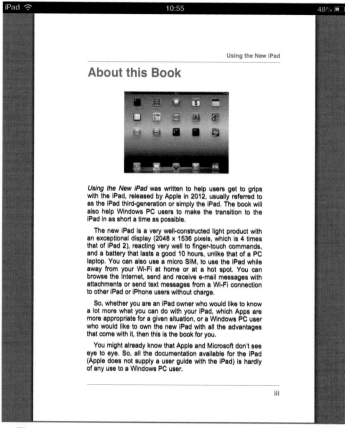

Fig. 7.14 The Opened SkyDrive PDF File on a Mobile Device.

8

Photos, Videos & Music

As we have seen earlier, in Windows 8 you can use either the **File Explorer** on the **Desktop** to navigate to the **Libraries** which point to the **Pictures**, **Videos** and **Music** folders or use the tiles provided on the **Start** screen which are used by mobile users (meaning mainly tablet users).

The Desktop Pictures Library

Window 8 in its **Desktop** mode provides a library for your photos, called the **Pictures** library. It is the default location for saving pictures and importing them from your digital camera.

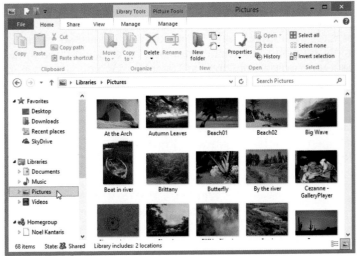

Fig. 8.1 Digital Photographs in the Pictures Folder.

I put most images I like in this folder, but keep my personal photos in sub-folders in another location on my hard drive.

The Picture Tools

As you can see in Fig. 8.1, the **Ribbon** tools are mostly greyed out until a picture is selected. When that is done, then you can **Delete** the selected picture, **Rename** it, **Move** it, **Copy** it, etc.

Fig. 8.2 shows the tools available to you on the **Ribbon** when a picture is selected and the **Picture Tools** button is tapped or clicked. You can now **Rotate** the selected picture to the left or right, **Set** it as background, or start a **Slide show**.

Fig. 8.2 Picture Tools.

Other **Ribbon** options allow you to **Share** selected pictures with friends and family, as was discussed earlier. It might be worth spending some time here, going through the various **Toolbar** options, to discover for yourself what is available.

The Windows Photo Viewer

To see a larger view of a picture, double-tap or double-click it to open it in the **Windows Photo Viewer**, as shown in Fig. 8.4 on the next page.

The **Toolbar** at the top of the **Windows Photo Viewer**, offers **File** options to **Make a Copy** or **Delete** a photo, **Print** or **Order Prints**, **Burn** a selection of photos to a data disc or use any of the listed programs in Fig. 8.3 to **Open** a photo for viewing or possibly editing.

Fig. 8.3 Program Options.

Fig. 8.4 The Windows Photo Viewer.

You can use the controls at the bottom of the **Viewer** to navigate through the current folder, view the pictures in your folder as a slide show, zoom in or out, rotate the image, and delete it from your hard disc.

Printing Photos

Selecting a picture in the **Viewer** and clicking the **Print** option in the **Share** tab, displays the window shown below.

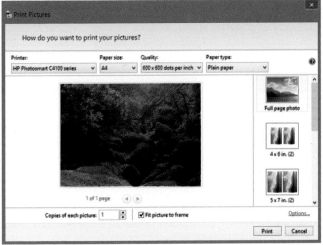

Fig. 8.5 The Print Pictures Window.

From here you can select the **Printer** to be used, **Paper size**, **Quality** of print, **Paper Type** and a variety of layouts for your pictures. All you have to do then is click the **Print** button.

The Photo App

Clicking the **Photos** tile on the **Start** screen, displays the screen shown in Fig. 8.6 below. Do note, however, that the picture on the **Photos** App tile shown to the left, changes because the photos in the **Pictures** library are shown as a live slide show, therefore what is shown here is bound to be different for you.

Fig. 8.6 Location of Photos for the Mobile User.

As you can see from the above display, all possible locations for photos are listed. The two main ones are the **Pictures library** and **SkyDrive**, while the other two, **Facebook** and **Flickr**, you can choose to **Hide** if your don't use these facilities. The **Devices** option allows you to fetch photos from attached devices or other computers on your network.

Next, tapping or clicking the photo in the **Pictures library**, displays a new enlarged screen, as shown in Fig. 8.7 on the next page.

Fig. 8.7 The Contents of the Pictures Library.

To reveal the options shown at the bottom of the above screen, either swipe upwards from the bottom of the screen or right-click. The options allow you to **Select** or **Delete** photos and start a **Slide show**. Another important option available here is to **Import** pictures from a camera.

Getting Photos from a Camera

There are many ways to import pictures from your digital camera (or phone) to your computer. Windows 8 makes the job extremely simple.

Fig. 8.8 Available Devices.

Once you have taken some photos, connect the camera (or phone) to your computer with the appropriate USB cable, switch the device on and tap or click the **Import** option in Fig. 8.7 to reveal the screen shown in Fig. 8.8. Selecting the **Portable Device**, displays Fig. 8.9 shown on the next page.

Fig. 8.9 Importing Pictures from a Portable Device.

Tapping or clicking the **Import** button pointed to above, starts importing the photos from your device into the **Pictures** folder. You can tell that this is so by the number of increased pictures now available in the **Pictures library**, as shown in Fig. 8.10.

Fig. 8.10 The Increased Number of Photos in the Pictures Library.

The number of photos available in the **Pictures library** has increased from 68 to 156. I did take rather a lot of photos on my holiday last summer!

If you now tap or click the encircled right-arrowhead pointed to in Fig. 8.10 above, a collage of your photos displays on your screen, as shown for my photo collection in Fig. 8.11 on the next page.

Fig. 8.11 A Collage of Imported Pictures.

By default, a new folder appears in the **Pictures library** and given a name made up from the date the pictures were imported, like **2012-11-03** in this case. You can see this by using the **File Explorer** on Windows 8 **Desktop** to look at the content of the **Pictures** library as shown here in Fig. 8.12.

Each photo in the folder is given a number which depends on your device. If you are happy with this, fine. If not you can spend a while renaming the folder and each picture.

Fig. 8.12 The Desktop Pictures Libraries Contents.

If you are like me and you don't import your photos into your computer often enough, then this is the time to use the desktop **File Explorer** to create new folders with appropriate names and sort your photos now rather than later, as it is very easy to forget where each photo was taken!

Scanning Photos

To import the images from paper photographs or slides into your computer you have to use a scanner. These are fairly cheap these days, in fact many printers include the ability to scan as well. To handle slides effectively though you need a special slide and negative scanner, but be warned these are not cheap!

Using the Windows Scan Facility

There are many ways to control a scanner using third party software but Windows 8 comes with its own program called **Windows Scan**, but you can only access it from the **Control Panel**.

With your scanner properly installed and turned on, you can open this program by tapping or clicking the **Desktop** tile on the **Start** screen, then opening the **Charms** bar shown in Fig. 8.13 and tapping or clicking the **Settings** charm. This opens the screen in Fig. 8.14 from which you can open the **Control Panel** shown in Fig. 8.15. In the **Control Panel**, tap or click the **Devices and Printers** entry pointed to in Fig. 8.15 below, to open a screen similar to that shown in Fig. 8.16 on the next page.

Fig. 8.13.

Fig. 8.14 The Settings Screen.

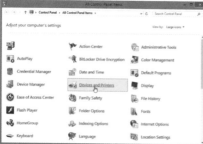

Fig. 8.15 The Control Panel Items.

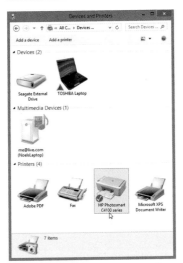

Fig. 8.16 The Devices and Printers Screen.

Touch and hold or right-click the default printer (which happens to be an all-in-one type) to open a menu of options as shown in Fig. 8.17 below.

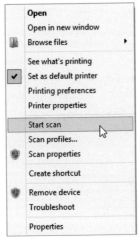

Fig. 8.17 The Right-click Menu.

From this menu of options you can set the **Scan Profiles** and **Scan Properties** and finally use the **Start scan** option to open the screen shown in Fig. 8.18.

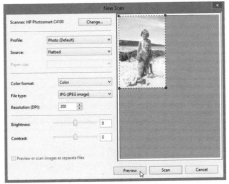

Fig. 8.18 The Preview of the Scanned Photo.

It is assumed that you have placed your photo on the scanner before using the **Preview** option so that you can limit the actual scan to the correct size by dragging the handles of the cropping tool. Having done so, you can use the **Scan** button to start the actual scan, after which the screen shown in Fig. 8.19 is displayed.

On this screen you can choose to **Review** or **Import** the scanned photo before pressing the **Next** button. Accepting the default setting and pressing the **Next** button, displays the screen shown

Fig. 8.19 The Import Pictures and Videos Screen.

in Fig. 8.20 where you can enter a name, add a tag, etc., before finally importing it into its own folder available to the **Pictures** library.

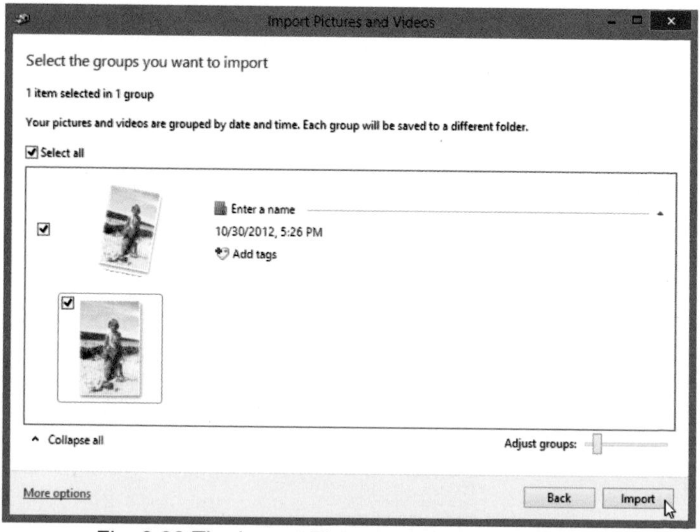

Fig. 8.20 The Import Pictures and Videos Screen.

The **Windows Scan** facility is not particularly intuitive, but it is easy enough to work with once you find out how to do it. The folder created and available to the **Pictures** library is similar to that created when you import pictures from a camera.

The Desktop Videos Library

In its **Desktop** mode, Windows 8 provides a library for your videos, called the **Videos** library. It is the default location for saving videos you might have received as attachments to e-mail messages, or imported from your video recorder.

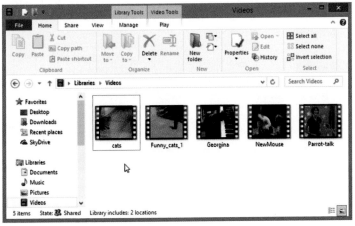

Fig. 8.21 The Videos Folder.

The Video Tools

In Fig. 8.21 above, the **Ribbon** tools are mostly greyed out

until a video is selected as shown in Fig. 8.22. When that is done, then you can **Delete** the selected video, **Rename** it, **Move** it, **Copy** it, etc., while other **Ribbon** options allow you to **Share** selected videos.

Fig. 8.22 Video Tools.

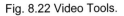

The Windows Video App

To start a video playing, double-tap or double-click it to open it in the **Windows Video** App, as shown in Fig. 8.23 below.

Fig. 8.23 The Windows Video App.

If you now revert to the **Start** screen of Windows 8, you'll see that the **Video** tile displays the name of the last video you played. In your case this is bound to be different, unless you have also named your video Georgina! Tapping or clicking the **Video** tile, displays a screen, part of which is shown in Fig. 8.24.

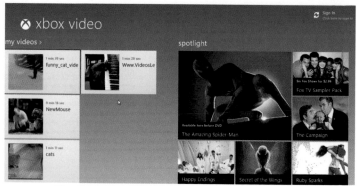

Fig. 8.24 Part of the Contents of the Video App.

On the left of the screen in Fig. 8.24 shown on the previous page, all the videos available to the **Videos** library are displayed (you will have to swipe with your finger to the right from the left edge of the screen or use the left arrow key on the keyboard to reveal them), while to the right of the screen thumbnails of videos, films or TV shows are displayed. When you tap or click one of these, a small window opens giving details of each item and giving you the opportunity to either purchase or rent a DVD or watch a trailer.

The Desktop Music Library

In its **Desktop** mode, Windows 8 provides a library for your music, called the **Music** library. It is the default location for saving music you might have downloaded, or imported from a CD.

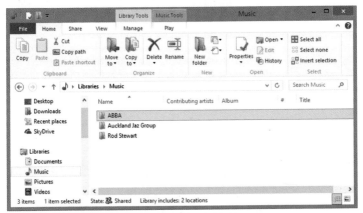

Fig. 8.25 The Music Folder.

The Music Tools

In Fig. 8.25 above, the **Ribbon** tools are mostly greyed out, just as they are for the other **Library** folders until a music folder or track is selected. When that is done, then you can **Delete** the selected music folder or track, **Rename** it, **Move** it, **Copy** it, etc., while other **Ribbon** options allow you to **Share** selected music with your **HomeGroup**.

The Windows Music App

To start a music track playing, double-tap or double-click it to open it in the **Windows Music** App, as shown in Fig. 8.26 below.

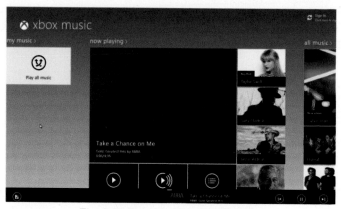

Fig. 8.26 The Windows Music App.

 If you now revert to the **Start** screen of Windows 8 and tap or click the **Music** tile, it displays a screen similar to that in Fig. 8.27 below.

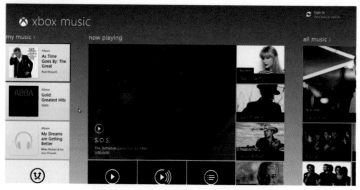

Fig. 8.27 Part of the Contents of the Music App.

To reveal the music in the **Music** library, swipe with your finger to the right from the left edge of the screen or press the left arrow key on the keyboard. It is even possible to find out the history associated with the group of musicians whose music you are playing at the time, as shown in Fig. 8.28.

Fig. 8.28 Biographical Information of Musicians.

To the right of the screen in Fig. 8.27 (see previous page), thumbnails of CD music covers are displayed. When you tap or click one of these, a small window opens giving details of the item and also giving you the opportunity to either buy the CD or play a music track, but for that to happen you must join the **xbox music** fraternity, as shown in Fig. 8.29 below.

Fig. 8.29 The Xbox Sign-in Screen.

The Xbox Player

Joining **xbox** requires you to give your date of birth (month and day – it seems to know the year)! Having done so and accepting certain conditions, you are given an **xbox** user 'gamertag', as shown in Fig. 8.30.

Fig. 8.30 The Xbox Welcome Screen.

Once you join **xbox**, you can listen to music tracks, as can be seen, but not heard, in Fig. 8.31.

Fig. 8.31 Playing an Xbox Music Track.

There is a lot more to **xbox** music playing, but I'm sure you'll be able to discover everything there is to know by yourself. Have fun!

9

Bing Maps

I hope you love maps as much as I do, because this chapter is dedicate to them. **Bing Maps** help you to see a 2D view of the world in **Road** view, **Aerial** view, **Bird's eye** view, **Streetside** view and finally a **3D** view. There are also **Venue** maps which provide a way of seeing the layout of a venue. You can use **Bing Maps** to plan your holiday, search for locations and addresses, find local services, get driving or walking directions, or just to enjoy looking at maps in their various views.

Bing Maps are available all over the world and its satellite imagery covers the entire planet, but at varying levels of resolution. You can approach **Bing Maps** either from the **Desktop** or by activating the **Maps** tile on the **Start** screen.

Bing Maps is an example of 'cloud computing' as you view maps in a Web browser and everything is downloaded from the Internet. The maps load quickly, especially if a reasonably fast Broadband connection is available, otherwise a little patience might be needed!

The Desktop Bing Maps Environment

Once your browser is open you can open **Bing Maps** in one of two ways. You can type **www.bing.com/maps** into the **Address** bar of your browser and press the **Enter** key, or you can tap or click the **Maps** link in the **Bing Navigation** bar of any **Bing** page, as shown in Fig. 9.1 below.

| WEB | IMAGES   VIDEOS   **MAPS**   NEWS   SEARCH HISTORY   MORE

Fig. 9.1 The Bing Navigation Bar.

With either of these methods the opening screen should look like that in Fig. 9.2 below.

Fig. 9.2 The Opening Screen for the UK Bing Maps.

You can now type a location, such as **_clifton bristol_** followed by **_map_**, to get a screen similar to that in Fig. 9.3 below.

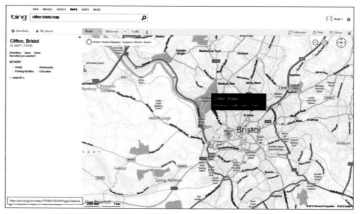

Fig. 9.3 A Search Screen for the UK Bing Maps Using a Location.

Tapping or clicking the **Zoom** link within the black oblong above, allows you to zoom in or out to see more or less detail of the area, while the **Directions** link changes the contents of the left panel in Fig. 9.3 so that you can type information for directions – more about this shortly.

Map Views

Depending on your location, there are different map views available in **Bing Maps**. These are controlled by the links at the top the map area, as shown in Fig. 9.2. When the mouse pointer hovers over the down-arrowheads of these two links, it displays other links, as shown in Fig. 9.4.

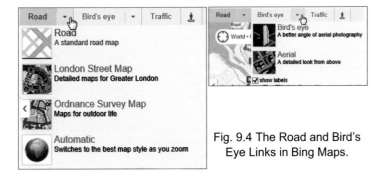

Fig. 9.4 The Road and Bird's Eye Links in Bing Maps.

You tap or click these links to change between the available views. In general, these links have the following effect:

Road – Displays a traditional style of map with a depiction of roads, borders, rivers, parks and lakes, etc.

Bird's eye – Displays aerial imagery of the same area. To show road and street names, select **Labels** on its drop-down options. The displayed images are not current and their quality depends on the locality.

Traffic – Displays visual traffic data for motorways and major trunk roads.

Ordnance Survey – This link on the drop-down **Roads** options in Fig. 9.4, displays **Ordnance Survey Maps** of the area. You'll need to zoom in or use a magnifying glass to see details!

Perhaps it might be worthwhile spending some time here to see the effect of all these links – far too many to give precise description of their effect. Experimenting in this case is by far the best way of finding out for yourself.

Searching for a Location

If you want to find details of a particular location you just search for it. This is a **bing** program after all! You can search for an address, city, town, airport, county, country or continent by typing details in the **Search** box and tapping or clicking the **Search** button, as shown below.

bing   st ives cornawall   🔍

Fig. 9.5 Entering a Search Address.

The result of this search is shown in Fig. 9.6 below. **Bing** jumped to a map of the Cornish town, placed a 'marker' on it and showed the search result in text in the left pane of the display.

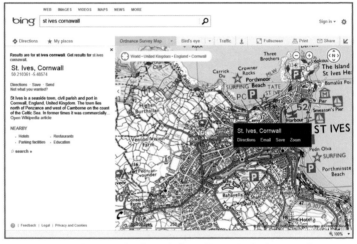

Fig. 9.6 The Result of a Search for a Town in Ordnance Survey Map View.

For specific addresses, entering them in the form of **Address, town, post code** usually gives the best results. You can also search for geographic features such as parks, mountains, lakes, etc., in the same way.

As shown in Fig. 9.6, the left pane can display a selection of **Nearby** options based on the current map location.

Tapping or clicking the **Restaurants** link displays a whole list of restaurants with their addresses and numerical markers showing their location on the map, as shown in Fig. 9.7.

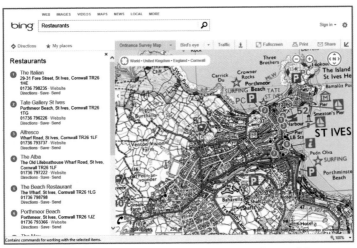

Fig. 9.7 The Result of a Search in Ordnance Survey View.

To revert to the previous view, tap or click the (**✗**) icon that appears just outside the top left corner of the map. Now you can look up other 'nearby' options.

Searching for Services

No matter where you are in the country, you can use **Bing Maps** to find the nearest business, educational or amusement service. Enter the appropriate words, followed by the words **in** or **near**, and the town, city or other location in the **Search** box. For example, typing *galleries in st ives cornwall* in the **Search** box and selecting **Bird's eye** view, displays the screen in Fig. 9.8, shown on the next page, when you tap or click the **Search** button.

Bing shows the results of the search in the left panel and a map of the area in the right panel, with markers linked to the results. You can now choose the gallery nearest the beach where you would like to spend the rest of the day!

Fig. 9.8 The Result of a Search for Galleries.

If you now tap or click a marker, either alongside an entry in the left panel or on the map, an info window opens with details of that facility, as shown in Fig. 9.9.

Fig. 9.9 The Info Window.

Navigating the Map Area

With **Bing Maps** you can change what shows in the map viewing area in two dimensions. You can pan the map (move it across the screen at the same scale), and you can zoom it in (to see a smaller area in more detail) or out (to see a larger area with less detail). You can navigate around a map using either your finger, the mouse or the supplied **Navigation** controls shown at the top-right corner in Fig. 9.8 above.

Using your finger to move around a map by simply touching the map and moving your finger in the direction you want to go. To zoom out you just place two fingers on the map and bring them together in a pinch movement and to zoom in you spread your fingers outwards (see Appendix A).

Using the mouse can also execute all the necessary operations easily and quickly. For example, to pan the map, just hold the left mouse button down to change the mouse pointer to a hand 🖑 which you use to drag the map around the screen. To zoom, just roll the mouse wheel away from you to zoom in, and towards you to zoom out. The zoom will centre on the pointer location on the map.

With these actions (fingers or mouse) you can almost instantly zoom out to view the whole Earth, as shown in Fig. 9.10, then move the pointer to a new location and zoom in again to the scale you need. You can also centre and zoom in on a location, by double-tapping or double-clicking it on the map.

Fig. 9.10 An Aerial View of the Whole Earth.

To pan the map, you use a finger or point with your mouse and left-click, then drag the map to move it to the direction you want to go.

You can use the two **Navigation** controls to zoom in ⊕ on the centre of the map, and ⊖ to zoom out.

If you prefer using the keyboard, you can zoom in and out with the **+** and **–** keys. You can pan left ⬅, right ➡, up ⬆, and down ⬇ with the arrow keys. The choice is yours!

Getting Directions

There are several ways in **Bing Maps** to get directions from one location to another. You can type a **from-to** statement into the search field, such as *from st ives cornwall to oxford*, and tap or click the **Search** button; you can tap or click the **Directions** link, enter a starting and ending location and tap or click the **Go** button or get directions from an info window (see Fig. 9.6).

The first method actually completes the operation as if you had used the second method, as shown in Fig. 9.11 below.

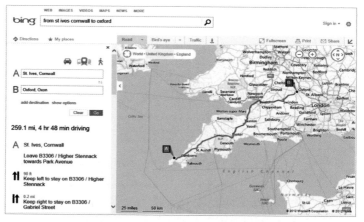

Fig. 9.11 Getting Driving Directions.

The program defaults to giving driving directions and the

recommended route appears on the map as a blue line with green and red markers at either end as shown in Fig. 9.11 above. **Bing Maps** gives a total distance, as shown on the left panel of Fig. 9.11 and suggests suitable routes in its detailed numbered directions (you might have to scroll down to see these), part of which is shown in Fig. 9.12.

Fig. 9.12 The Suggested Route.

If you tap or click on a route section in the left panel, an enlarged map opens, as shown in Fig. 9.13.

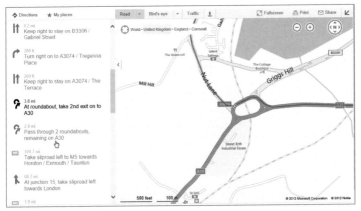

Fig. 9.13 Street View Information for a Section.

The **Bird's eye** view of the above map is worth seeing, as displayed below in Fig. 9.14.

Fig. 9.14 Bird's Eye View for a Section of the Map.

When you study the proposed route on the map you may find you want to alter it. That's no problem with **Bing Maps**. You can just drag a point on the blue directions line to any location on the map. As an example, I decided to take the scenic route to Oxford, as shown in Fig. 9.15, but doing so has increased the journey time by 1 hour from the originally suggested route, even though it is 1 mile less!

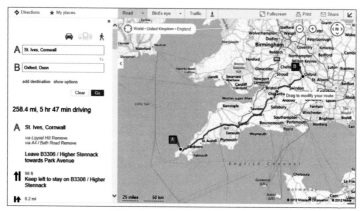

Fig. 9.15 The Scenic Route.

Public Transport

Depending on where you are, the **Public Transport** feature of **Bing Maps** may let you map your trip using train, bus and coach transport. If transit information is available when you search for directions between start and end locations in **Bing Maps**, the **Public Transport** option 🚊 will appear under the **Directions** option, as in Fig. 9.16 below.

Fig. 9.16 A Set of Public Transport Directions in Road View.

The times of departure of the various methods of public transport are given in the left panel. Again you'll have to scroll down to see these. To plan your trip in the future, click the down-arrowheads and select a new date and time.

This feature could be very useful, but until much better coverage is available in the UK you would be best using it with care.

Walking for Charity

If you really want to walk from St. Ives, Cornwall to Oxford, then you might as well do it for charity. The map below gives you precise directions. It will only take 79 hours and 5 minutes. Some brisk walk!

Fig. 9.17 Walking the Distance in Road View.

However, since the last Windows 8 update, instead of getting the above instructions, you get the message:

> Walking directions are not available for a route of this length. Try driving directions instead.

Obviously someone who does not believe in walking for charity has decided that to walk this distance is rather unhealthy (unless you use the driving directions and walk on the motorway instead)! If you change the destination from Oxford to Clifton, Bristol, the program accepts this as a reasonable distance to walk, a mere 178.2 miles, taking 57 hours and 22 minutes. I wonder who measured this walk so precisely!

Printing Bing Maps

You can print both **Road** view maps and **Bird's eye** view maps with their direction information in **Bing Maps**. With the map area you want to print on the screen, tap or click the **Print** 🖶 icon at the top right of the map area to display an additional screen in which you can choose to print the **Map and text**, **Map only** or **Text only**. With the first option, under the main map you also get detailed maps of the start and end destinations of your choice, even though these do not display on the screen – only the directions appear on the preview screen. Fig. 9.18 shows a scanned display of the printout.

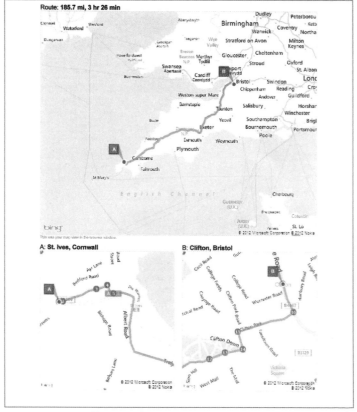

Fig. 9.18 Scanned Direction Maps.

Streetside View

 If you tap or click the **Streetside** view ⬆ icon at the top of the map area, the cursor changes to a blue 'Peg Man' as shown here, with the map itself displaying blue areas within which a **Streetside** view is available (Fig. 9.19).

Fig. 9.19 Available Streetside View Area Coverage.

Europe, for the present, has only four areas in the UK and two in France. The moment you move the 'Peg Man' to one of these areas the screen changes to that of Fig. 9.20.

Fig. 9.20 The Microsoft Silverlight Installation.

Tapping or clicking the **Start the map app**, the **Silverlight** App is installed within half a minute and the screen changes to one similar to that in Fig. 9.21.

Fig. 9.21 A Streetside View Display.

To use the **Streetside** view effectively, it is best to exit the above view, then use **bing** to search for a known address.

For example, let us search for the **Streetside** view of Royal York Crescent in Clifton, Bristol. To achieve this, do the following:

- Start **Maps** in **Internet Explorer**.

- Type the search criteria given above in **bing** and tap or click the search button.

- When the road map of the area is displayed on your screen, press the **Search** ₚ button.

- When **bing** finds the location, press the **Streetside** View ⬇ icon to change the pointer to the blue 'Peg Man'.

Placing this on the desired location displays the screen shown in Fig. 9.22 on the next page.

Fig. 9.22 A Streetside View of the Royal York Crescent in Clifton.

There are several things to remember when you display a location in **Streetside** view. These are:

- To move to a required position on a street, drag the street to the focus in the small preview window at the top-right corner of the display, not the other way round.

- To change the viewing direction use the curved arrows on the navigation control.

- To zoom in or out, tap or click the ⊕ or ⊖ buttons.

- As you move the mouse pointer within **Streetside** view, you'll notice that the 'Peg Man' changes its stance; upright when you are following a road or pointing right or left. Tapping or clicking the latter, moves what you see in the direction pointed by the 'Peg Man'.

- Sometimes the pointer changes to a magnifying glass with either a **+** or a **-** sign on it. Tapping or clicking such a pointer zooms you in or out.

Again, the only way of getting familiar with **Streetside** view is by trying to use it and experimenting with the pointer.

Once you have found the area you want to explore with **Streetside** view, tap or click the **Enter full screen mode** button to view a larger **Streetside** view area. To return **Streetside** view to its previous size, tap or click the **Exit full screen mode** button.

To exit **Streetside** view, tap of click the ← Exit button which returns you to **Road** view.

To see some really spectacular photos of the Royal York Crescent, use **bing** to search for it, then tap or click the **BING APP** pointed to in Fig. 9.23.

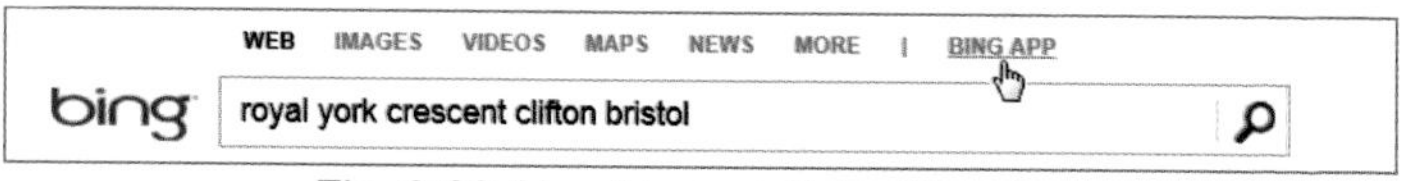

	WEB	IMAGES	VIDEOS	MAPS	NEWS	MORE		BING APP
bing	royal york crescent clifton bristol							🔍

Fig. 9.23 About to Install the Bing App.

After accepting to install this App, the collage of photos shown in Fig. 9.24 appers on your screen.

Fig. 9.24 A Collage of Streetside View Photos of The Royal York Crescent in Clifton, Bristol.

What is shown above is only the first page of several pages of these photos!

Sharing Maps

If you tap or click the link pointed to in Fig. 9.25 at the top of the **bing Maps** main window (you might have to increase the width of the window to see it), you can e-mail the current map or directions to a friend or colleague.

Fig. 9.25 The Share Link.

This **Share** button when clicked displays the small window shown in Fig. 9.26.

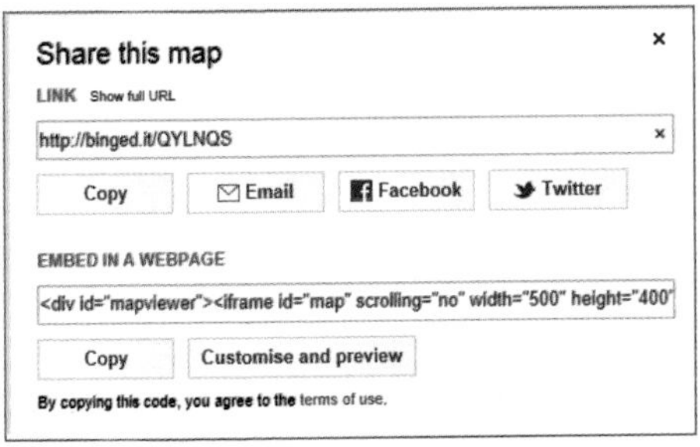

Fig. 9.26 The Link Window.

From here you can either have a copy of the URL inserted in the body of an e-mail message when you click the **send** button, or copy and paste the HTML code to embed the current map into a Web page. You can then either e-mail directly to a friend, or make the information available in **Facebook** or **Twitter**.

Traffic View

Bing Maps has an exciting feature, that provides traffic data for the motorways and major A roads in England, Scotland, and parts of Europe.

In Fig. 9.27 on the next page, I show the **Road** map view of a specific area, Clifton in Bristol, so that you can compare this map with the **Traffic** version of the same area.

Whatever map view you are in, if you tap or click the **Traffic** link, the parts of motorways and trunk roads that are subject to traffic hold ups will be overlayed with colour, as shown in Fig. 9.28, also shown on the next page.

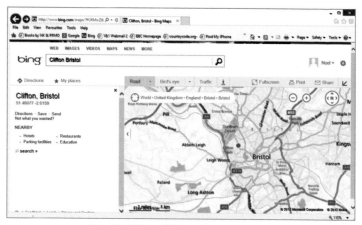

Fig. 9.27 Road View Around Clifton.

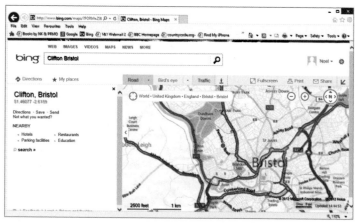

Fig. 9.28 Traffic View Around Clifton.

If your route shows red, it's stop-and-go for you, while green means it is probably clear, as shown here. This is a very good feature when you are about to start your journey, but not so good if you are driving at the time, unless you have a tablet device with you! The map was updated only 10 min ago from writing.

When you are finished, click the **Traffic** link again to deselect it and turn off the feature.

The Maps App

If you tap or click the **Maps** App tile on the Windows 8 **Start** screen, what displays first on your screen is a map of your location (if you have given your permission to be located). Swipping upwards from the bottom of the screen or right-clicking, displays the **bing Toolbar** at the bottom of the screen, as shown in Fig. 9.29.

Fig. 9.29 The Bing Toolbar.

From here, you can **Add a pin** to the map, **Show traffic**, choose a **Map style**, display **My location**, obtain **Directions** and **Find** places or services.

If you tap or click on **Map style**, you'll see that the choice is confined to either **Road view** or **Aerial view**, while the **Directions** tool opens a window on the top-right of the map screen as shown here in Fig. 9.30. Note that the program remembers the destinations you used when using **bing** from the **Desktop**. The only difference is that the starting point of your journey is assumed to be from your current location, although you can easily change this.

Fig. 9.30 The Directions Window.

A similar window is displayed if you tap or click **Find** on the toolbar, which also includes a list of suggested places taken from previous use of **bing**. If you type, say King's College Cambridge, you are told to refine your search. However, if you first search for **University Cambridge**, then tap or click the **Find** tool once more, but now type **King's College**, you are taken to the correct place.

In Fig. 9.31 overleaf, King's College is displayed on **Aerial View**, but zoomed in so that its features are shown very clearly. Try it for yourself.

Fig. 9.31 Aerial View of King's College Cambridge.

To change the view to **Traffic**, you must first zoom out before the App can display what you want. You cannot print anything from within this App, but you can go to the **Desktop** version of **bing** and get to the same display as the above before printing. Strangely enough, searching for King's College Cambridge on **bing**'s **Desktop** version, finds the location instantly!

As usual, the only way to find out how this App works is to try it. Have fun!

10

News, Finance & Weather

The News App

These days every newspaper and other news source has a Web site showing a continuously updated online version of its news and story contents. We all like to know what is happening and where.

Windows 8 goes one step further, it shows live content of news continuously as it happens as shown in Fig. 10.1 below.

Fig. 10.1 The Top Story in Today's News.

Although it is possible to use **bing** to search for news, it is not as satisfying visually as using the **News** App, so it is not worth spending time on it.

News Layout

You can swipe to the left or use the right cursor key on the keyboard to see more sections under headings like **Headlines**, **UK**, **World**, **Entertainment**, **Business** and **Sport**. In other words, everything to keep you occupied for quite a long time.

Each section has several topics within it, as shown in Fig. 10.2.

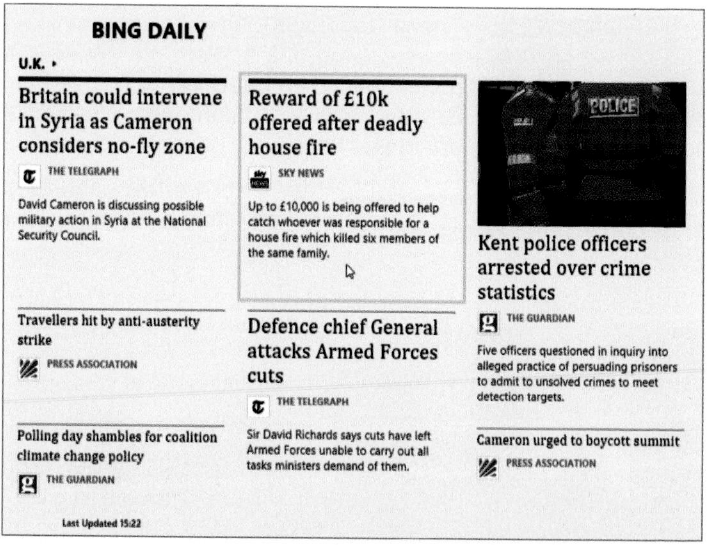

Fig. 10.2 Topics within a Section of Today's News.

As you can see the last update was about 10 minutes ago from the time of writing this sentence, so you do get the very up-to-date news.

As the mouse pointer passes over a topic, lines around the topic indicate that if you left-click, the full story of that particular topic will display. Touching a topic with a finger, also opens the topic in full screen.

Once a topic is selected, swiping upwards from the bottom of the screen or right-clicking the mouse, displays options as shown in Fig. 10.3 on the next page.

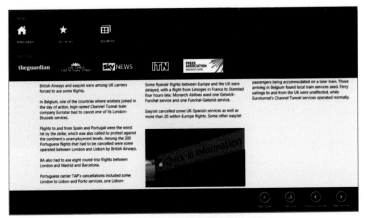

Fig. 10.3 Options within Today's News.

The tools at the bottom of the screen, allow you to change the **Text style** and **Text size**, go to the **Previous article** or to the **Next article**.

News from Specific Sources

At the top of the screen, second row, are icons to **Featured** articles from specific sources. These icons appear at the top of your screen whether you have selected a topic or not. To see articles from, say, the **Guardian**, just tap or click the **theguardian** icon, to display a screen similar to that in Fig. 10.4 below.

Fig. 10.4 Today's News from a Specific Source.

News is 'untouched by human hand' as the stories, headlines and photos you see on it are selected entirely by computer algorithms, based on factors like how often and where a story appears online. The grouping and ranking of stories depends on such things as titles, text, and publication time.

The three icons at the very top of the screen, also shown here, have the following functions:

- Touching or clicking the **Bing Daily** icon, displays the screen that appears first when you tap or click the **News** tile on the **Start** screen. It 'Homes' to the very beginning of the **News**.

- Touching or clicking the **Sources** icon, displays a screen similar to that in Fig. 10.5.

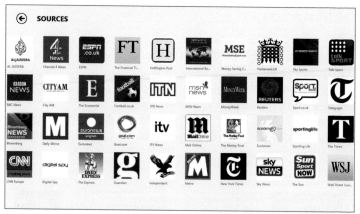

Fig. 10.5 All the Available News Sources.

These are the sources from where you can select to obtain news. For example, tapping or clicking on the **BBC News** icon, displays everything available on this source at the time, as shown in Fig. 10.6 on the next page. Obviously this is not what you'll see, because by the time you look at the BBC site the news would have changed!

Fig. 10.6 Current News on the BBC.

- Touching or clicking the **My News** icon, displays a screen similar to that in Fig. 10.7.

Fig. 10.7 The My News Content.

Microsoft provides this page as your first choice of **My News** content, but as you can see, you can add to it by tapping or clicking the icon with the **+** sign. Doing so displays the screen in Fig. 10.8.

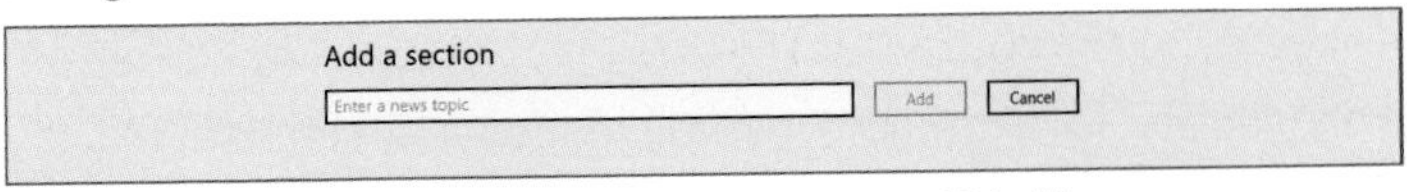

Fig. 10.8 Adding to the Content of My News.

For example, if you type **European News** as your choice of news and press the **Add** button, then a screen similar to that in Fig. 10.9 will display.

Fig. 10.9 The Latest Content in My News.

If you want to remove a section of news, highlight it and use the **Remove** button also pointed to in Fig. 10.10.

Fig. 10.10 Removing a Section from the Content in My News.

This facility is extremely useful, as you customise exactly what you want to see from the news of the day.

The Finance App

If you have a financial or business interest in company stocks and shares, mutual funds and international currency rates, then the **Finance** App will be useful to you. If not, you can probably skip the rest of this chapter. Windows 8's **bing Finance** offers an easy way to search for share prices, mutual fund details and financial information on publicly listed companies. All the things pensions are made up from!

To access the **bing Finance** page, simply tap or click the **Finance** tile on the **Start** screen to open the first screen with the most recent news on finance, as shown in Fig. 10.11.

Fig. 10.11 Today's Bing Opening Finance Page.

The opening page should look similar to the one above, but obviously with different content. To the right of the page current topics under titles such as **Market** (you can see part of this on the right of the screen above), **Watchlist**, **News** and 'Currencies' **Across the Market**.

If you have obtained any quotes, these will be listed under **Watchlist**. Fig. 10.12 on the next page, displays what appears if you have not added to the list yet. You can add to or remove from the suggested list.

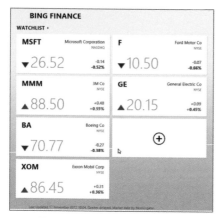

Fig. 10.12 Items on Watchlist.

To search for prices of mutual funds or stock market companies, first tap or click the **Add** ⊕ button to open the screen in Fig. 10.13. Next, use either their names or their ticker symbols and start typing. Bing is very clever here with its *Autosuggest* feature.

Fig. 10.13 Adding to the Watchlist.

As you type in the first part of a name a list instantly appears with suggestions on what you might be looking for, as shown in Fig. 10.14 below. You just tap or click the option you want in the list, the ticker symbol is automatically placed in the **Watchlist**, and the home page changes to a detailed page of data on the Company you searched for, as shown in Fig. 10.15 on the next page.

Add to Watchlist

sai				×	Add	Cancel
0M9X	Saint Gobain Oberland AG	Stock	London			
0NWY	Saipem Spa	Stock	London			
0NWZ	Saipem Spa	Stock	London			
SBRY	J Sainsbury PLC	Stock	London			
COD	Saint-Gobain	Stock	London			

Fig. 10.14 Autosuggestion.

Company Summary

This gives an overview of the current UK financial situation of the selected company, with access to the main news story on the company displayed on the right of the screen of Fig. 10.15.

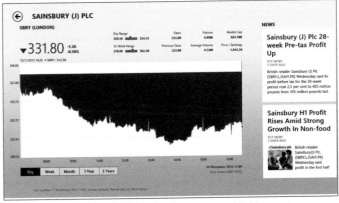

Fig. 10.15 SBRY Day Performance Chart.

Swiping to the left reveals screens which include summaries on **Key Statistics** and **Fund Ownership Trends**, as shown in Fig. 10.16 below.

Funds	Fund Rating	Buying/Selling Trend	% Change
CF TY Intl Equity (Ebias) A Acc	★★★★★	Buying	100.00%
AEGON Europees Mix Fonds	★★★★★	Selling	-99.85%
AEGON Wereldwijd Aandelen Fonds	★★★★★	Selling	-99.26%
Optimum Ibbotson Balanced Growth Plus	★★★★★	Buying	91.66%
Optimum Ibbotson Cons Gr Plus	★★★★★	Buying	86.35%
Legal and General - L&G CAF UK Equitrack	★★★★★	Buying	84.56%
Parworld Track UK	★★★★★	Selling	-81.96%
Smith & Williamson Enterprise Fund	★★★★★	Buying	80.00%
Smith & Williamson UK Equity Gr Trust	★★★★★	Buying	75.00%
JHVIT International Index Trust	★★★★★	Selling	-73.99%

SAINSBURY (J) PLC

FUND OWNERSHIP TRENDS

As compared to fund's last portfolio date

Fig. 10.16 Performance of Related Companies.

Removing Companies from the Watchlist

To remove an entry from the **Watchlist** select it, then either swipe from the bottom edge of the screen upwards or right-click to reveal the **Tools** bar at the bottom of the screen and tap or click the **Remove** 🔄 button, as shown in Fig. 10.17.

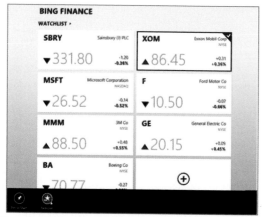

Fig. 10.17 Removing a Company from the Watchlist.

Market News

News stories on **bing Finance** are accessed by swiping left to display the next screen from the **Watchlist** page. The home page shows the **Top stories** for the **Market** generally, as shown in Fig. 10.18.

Fig. 10.18 Market News Home Page.

Tracking Currencies and Commodities

Bing Finance offers data on how leading currencies are performing against each other. You'll find a list of currencies on **Across the Market** page (swipe left to the penultimate screen) to display a page similar to that in Fig. 10.19.

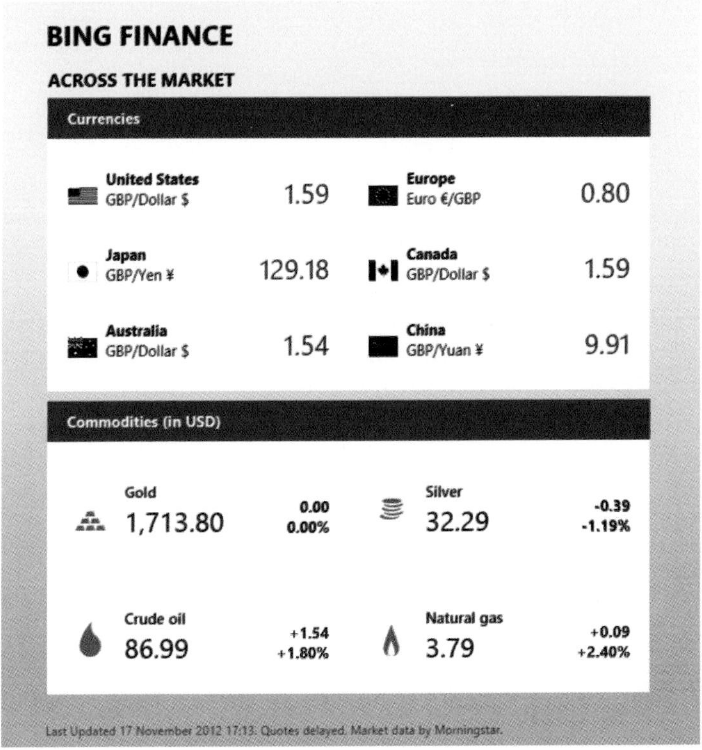

Fig. 10.19 Currencies and Price of Commodities.

Clicking on a link such as **EURO €/GBP**, displays a page of current exchange rates for this and the other main financial currencies, as shown in Fig. 10.20 on the next page.

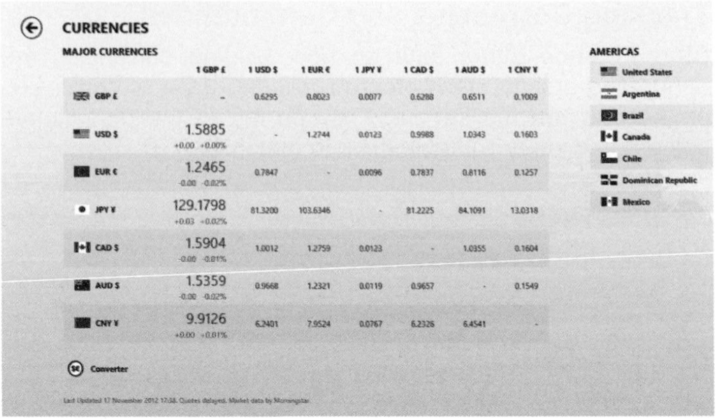

Fig. 10.20 Currency Exchange Rates and Conversion.

There is also a very useful currency converter at the bottom left corner of the above page. Tapping or clicking its icon displays the screen shown in Fig. 10.21.

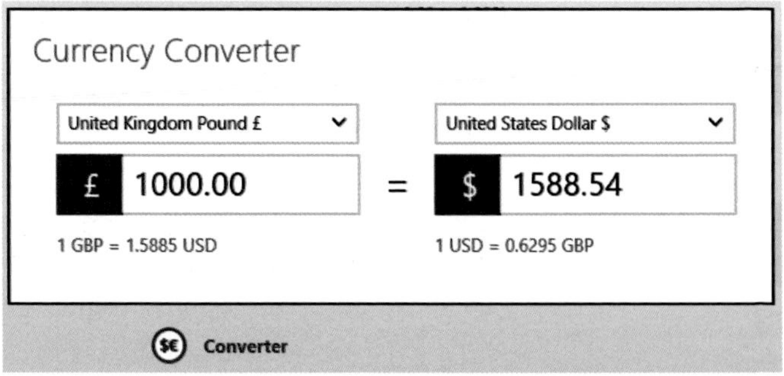

Fig. 10.21 The Currency Converter.

You can use the down-arrowheads to select from a list of currencies which gives you an instant conversion rate.

* * *

Good luck using **bing Finance**, it certainly is quite fascinating. One could spend hours trying to become a millionaire, but be careful not to spend what you haven't got!

The Weather App

These days the weather is an integral part of news and finance. It certainly has a profound effect on both of these, so I decided to include it in this chapter.

Tapping or clicking the **Weather** App displays the following screen.

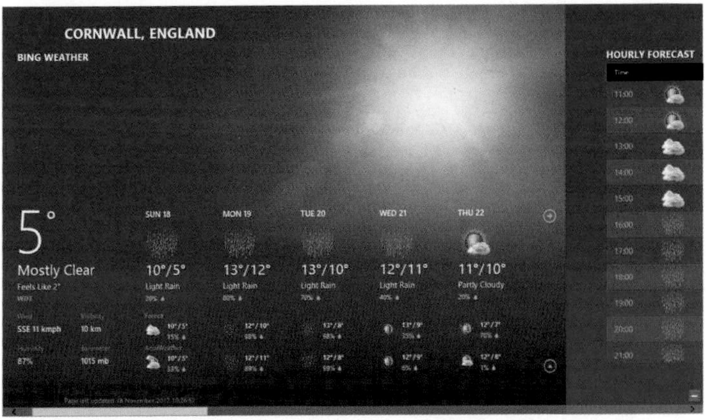

Fig. 10.22 The Weather at your Locality.

The **Weather** App allows you to customise it and include other localities, but to begin with it senses where you are, so what is displayed when you first start it is related to your area.

As you can see from the opening screen, there are additional screens which can be displayed by either swiping to the left or using the slider with the mouse. The slider only displays when your mouse pointer is placed near the bottom of the screen.

Additional tools can be displayed on the screen by swiping from the bottom edge of the screen upwards or right-clicking with the mouse. The usual tools appear at the bottom of the screen on the **Toolbar**, while at the top of the screen various options are displayed, as shown in Fig. 10.23 on the next page.

Fig. 10.23 The Weather Toolbar and Options.

Fig. 10.24 Items on Watchlist.

On the top of the screen you can use the **Places** ★ button to open your **Favourites**. As you can see, I have already added an extra place by using the ⊕ button. In fact, the buttons at the left of the **Toolbar** at the bottom of the screen only change to what appears in Fig. 10.24 after you have created an extra location and tapped or clicked the **Current Location** ⊚ button.

Other **Toolbar** buttons can be used on selected sites to **Remove** them from **Favourites**, **Pin to Start** screen and even change displayed temperatures from Celsius to Fahrenheit.

A rather useful page in the **Weather** App gives you **Historical** information on monthly temperatures, rainfall and snow days, well worth examining these. Finally, if you are interested in **World Weather**, you can look at it from the comfort of your home by simply tapping or clicking the ⊠ button!

11

Media Player & Media Center

Both **Media Player** and **Media Center** have been designed to handle all your digital media content, such as digital music, videos, photos, recorded TV shows and streamed Internet media.

As you have seen earlier, media files are saved by default to the **Music** and **Video** libraries automatically by the media programs described here. The **Media Player** is available to both Windows 8 and Windows 8 Pro, but not to Windows RT.

However, Microsoft has decided to remove DVD playback from Windows 8, as the Operating System was primarily designed for ultrabooks, tablets and hybrid PCs that lack optical drives. So now **Windows Media Player** can only play your music and your videos and display your pictures.

Note: If you want to play DVDs on your computer's optical drive, you must download and install **Media Center** which is only available to you if you upgrade from Windows 8 to Windows 8 Pro Pack, then apply to Microsoft for a product 'key' to allow you to download and install **Media Center** (free until 31/1/2013).

The Desktop Windows Media Player

The **Desktop** Windows **Media Player** is the main media 'workhorse' in Windows 8. It has been around for a few years now. It provides a good-looking, intuitive and easy-to-use desktop interface for you to play the digital media files stored on your computer, or on CDs, or other external storage devices.

You can organise your digital media collection, rip music from your CDs to the computer and burn CDs of your favourite music, so you can play them on your home system or in your car.

It also lets you sync (synchronise) digital media files to a large range of portable media devices (but not Apple iPods and iPads unfortunately), and encourages you to shop for digital media content online. In other words, with **Media Player** you can play your audio and video material, view it, organise it, or sync it, but not your DVDs.

Searching for the Media Player

By default, the **Windows Media Player** is not pinned on the **Taskbar**, where it would be convenient to have it. So, the first thing to do is find it using the **Search** charm, as shown in the composite screen dump in Fig. 11.1 below.

Fig. 11.1 Searching for Media Player.

First, swipe from the right edge of the screen towards the left or place the mouse pointer at the top-right corner of the screen, to reveal the **Charms** bar, then tap or click the **Search** charm as shown on the right of Fig. 11.1. This opens a separate screen, shown on the left of the above display, where you can type your search criteria.

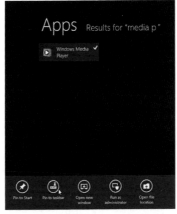

Fig. 11.2 Finding an App.

As you type, a number of Apps appear on the screen which reduce in number as you continue typing. Eventually the App you are looking for is displayed on the screen.

To pin this App on the **Taskbar**, touch and hold or right-click it to display the options **Toolbar** at the bottom of the screen, the left part of which is shown in Fig. 11.2. Next, tap or click the **Pin to taskbar** button to complete the operation.

Starting Media Player

By default, tapping or clicking the **Windows Media Player** button on the **Taskbar** will open the program.

Media Player displays many views onto your media, but if you have a CD in your optical drive it might, when started, look something similar to that in Fig. 11.3 below.

Fig. 11.3 A Player View of a Music CD.

Ripping from Audio CDs

The tracks and songs on an inserted CD will not show in your **Library** unless you 'rip' them from the CD. This is not as destructive as it sounds. It simply means copying tracks from the CD to the library on your computer's hard disc, so that you can listen to them whenever you want to.

The tracks ready to be ripped from the inserted audio CD (see Fig. 11.3 on the previous page) display in the **Details** pane with the album art and all the album tracks named and selected ready to be copied to your library.

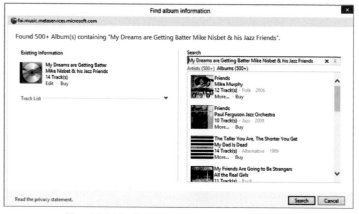 If the **Media Player** does not recognise the CD automatically it will show as an **Unknown album**. It is usually easy to correct this by touching and holding or right-clicking the default album artwork graphic shown here and selecting the **Find album info** option. In this case the artist's name and the album title are known and are automatically inserted in the **Search** box (you might have to type this information, if it isn't picked up automatically), then tap or click the **Search** button and hopefully select the correct album from the list offered (Fig. 11.4)

Fig. 11.4 Finding Album Information for a CD.

Finally, after you have made the correct selection, tap or click the **Next** button, check that the track information is correct and select **Finish** to accept the info shown.

By default, Windows **Media Player** rips to **.wma** format with CD quality encoding. This is good enough for me, but if you want to change these settings click **Rip settings** on the **Button** bar and choose **More options**.

If there are any tracks that you don't want to rip, clear the check box next to them (Fig. 11.3). When you are ready, click the **Rip CD** ✦ button on the **Button** bar to start the process. You will be warned about licence requirements, etc., after which ripping begins.

By default the selected tracks are copied to the **Music** library on your PC with folders added and labelled with the name of the artist or group.

While the ripping operation is in progress you can see exactly what is going on by looking at the **Rip status** column. You can listen to the CD while you are ripping it, so you needn't get too bored. By the time you listen to one track, the whole process would have completed.

To cancel ripping at any time, just tap or click the **Stop rip** ⊙ button. Once you have done one CD you will find it very easy to rip your whole collection.

Monitoring Folders

After removing the CD from optical drive, and restarting the **Media Player**, it automatically searches the default folders included in the libraries on your computer. If you ever change the files in the **Music**, **Pictures** and **Videos** libraries, the **Media Player** will automatically update what is available the next time it starts up. To build your media library, you can also include folders in the libraries from other locations on your computer or external devices, such as portable hard drives, or storage devices.

Player View Modes

Media Player lets you toggle between two main view modes. The **Player Library** shown in Fig. 11.5 on the next page, which gives you control of all the **Player**'s features, and a **Now Playing** mode, shown in Fig. 11.6 also on the next page, which gives a simplified view ideal for playback.

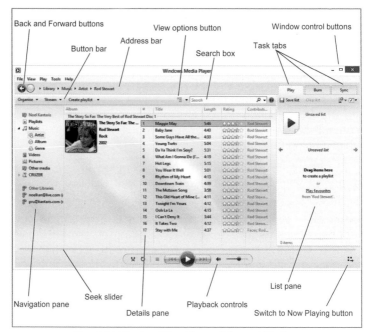

Fig. 11.5 Parts of the Player Library Window.

To move between these modes click the **Switch to Now Playing** button, or from the **Media Player**, the **Switch to Library** button in the upper-right corner pointed to in Fig. 11.6.

Fig. 11.6 Now Playing Mode.

When you tap or click an item, such as **Music**, in the **Navigation** pane it lists your media content in the **Details** pane. Tapping or clicking on **Artist** will list your music files by artist and double-tapping or double-clicking on a CD icon, lists the tracks on that CD. Double-tapping or double-clicking on a track name will start it playing in the **Media Player**.

There are three different viewing options in the **Details** pane, chosen from a drop-down menu by tapping or clicking the arrow next to the **View options** button, shown here in Fig. 11.7, or by just tapping or clicking the button itself repeatedly until you get the view you want. Do examine these views to see which you prefer.

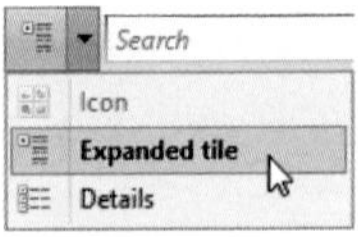

Fig. 11.7 The View Options.

Searching a Library

When you want to find a specific artist, album title or song name, you can simply type a search string in the **Search** box as shown in Fig. 11.8. For example, typing **help** immediately presents results of the search (top-half of Fig. 11.8) and tapping or clicking on it, displays another screen with the actual details (bottom-half of Fig. 11.8) naming the **Beatles** album and the track number in this example.

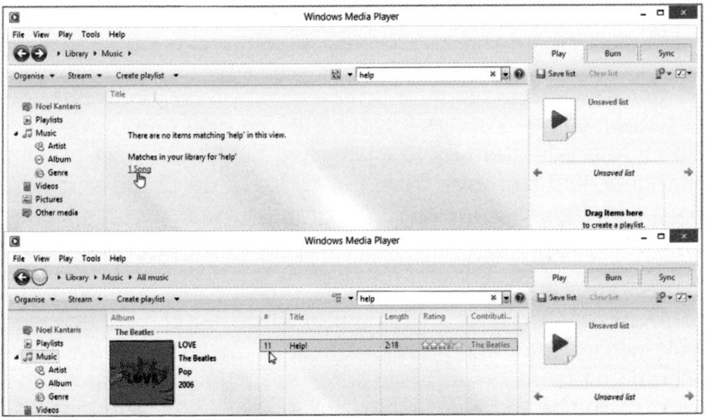

Fig. 11.8 Searching for Specific Music.

Double-tapping or double-clicking on the track number plays the song. It is that simple!

The **Playback Controls** are always visible at the bottom of the **Player Library** and their functions are similar to a normal CD player. In any case, you can always find out what each control button does by lightly touching it or hovering the mouse pointer over it – its function appears in a text pop-up.

Using Playlists

A **Playlist** is a saved list of media items (such as songs) which appears in your Library on the left side in the

Fig. 11.9 List Pane.

Navigation pane. Creating, saving and editing **Media Player Playlists** of your favourite tracks is very easy. You do it in the **List** pane shown in Fig. 11.9 which is opened when you tap or click the **Play** tab.

If there are items in the list, use **Clear list** to remove them. To name a new **Playlist** tap or click the *Unsaved list* text item pointed to in Fig. 11.9, type a name, say **Favourites**, and click the **Save list** button. You should do this whenever you make changes. To add songs to the **Playlist** find them in your **Player Library** and just drag and drop them into the new list.

Once you have songs in your **Playlist**, you can move them about and edit them by touching and holding or right-clicking and choosing **Remove from list** or **Move up** or **Move down**. You can also reorder them by dragging and dropping them within the list.

For more options, click the **List options** button in the top-right corner of the **List** pane. From here, you can sort your list according to attributes such as artist name, title, album and length. This is similar to sorting songs by columns. Using **Shuffle list** rearranges the items in your **Playlist** in a random order. Once you have created and saved a list it shows in the **Playlists** item in the **Navigation** pane, as shown in Fig. 11.10.

Fig. 11.10 Playing the Favourite List.

Burning CDs

With **Media Player** you can burn, or create, CD-R and CD-RW type CDs, as long as you have a suitable recorder on your PC. To begin, insert a blank CD into your disc drive. If the **AutoPlay** window pops up, choose **Burn an audio CD using Windows Media Player**. If not simply open Windows **Media Player** as usual.

You burn a CD in the **Burn List** pane shown in Fig. 11.11. This should appear automatically, but if it doesn't just tap or click the **Burn** tab.

If there are items in the list, click **Clear list** to remove them. To name the new disc tap or click the **Burn list** item pointed to in Fig. 11.11, and type a name for it. This will show up on CD players that support CD text.

Fig. 11.11 The Burn List Pane.

As with a **Playlist**, to add songs to the **Burn** list, find them in your **Player Library** and drag and drop them into the new list.

If necessary you next choose the **Disc Type** you want to burn. There are three different types of discs you can burn:

Audio CD – These hold about 80 minutes of music, are readable by computers and are playable in any CD player. This type was automatically selected in the example above.

Data CD – These hold about 700 MB of data, are readable by computers and CD players that support playback of digital audio files. They are not playable on standard CD players.

Data DVD – These hold about 4 GB of data and are readable by DVD players that support playback of digital audio files. They are primarily intended to be readable by computers. In Windows 8 you need to install **Media Center**.

To choose the type of disc to burn, click the **Burn options** button in the top right corner and choose from the drop-down menu. You can also adjust other options by clicking **More burn options** which opens the **Media Player Options** box shown below.

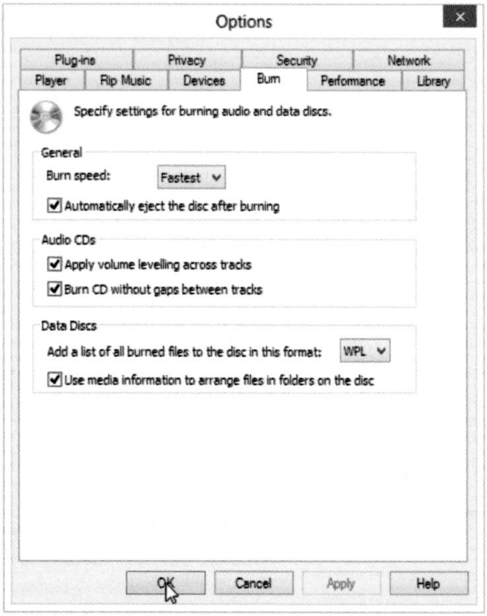

Fig. 11.12 Windows Media Player Options Box.

When you are happy with your settings, tap or click **Apply** and **OK**, followed by the **Start burn** button.

When the burn begins, the status is shown in a green bar at the top of the **Burn List**. Tapping or clicking the blue text link below it lets you see the status of each individual track.

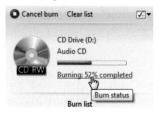

Quite a straightforward operation which you can use to create audio CDs to use in your car on those long boring journeys abroad!

Fig. 11.13 Burn Status.

Windows Media Center

 Up to now, most people avoided using Windows **Media Center**, particularly since Windows **Media Player** used to serve their needs with playing films on DVDs. Not anymore!

With Windows 8 your DVD playback requires the use of **Media Center**, which you have to download and install on your computer as mentioned at the beginning of this chapter.

Windows **Media Center** is designed to serve as a home-entertainment hub for the living-room TV and was first included in various versions of Windows XP (Media Center edition), Windows Vista (Home Premium and Ultimate), all editions of Windows 7 (except Starter and Home Basic), and now in Windows 8 Pro, but as an add-on.

If you have a TV tuner for your computer, using Windows **Media Center** allows you to watch, pause, and record live TV, if not, there is still Internet TV which offers online shows and movies. But you can also use **Media Center** to play your videos and music and display your pictures from your computer's local hard drives, optical drives and from networks. It can then sort them by name, date, tags and other file attributes.

Adding and Installing Media Center

To download and add either Windows 8 **Pro Pack** or Windows 8 **Media Center Pack** to Windows 8, swipe inwards from the right edge of the screen or point to the top-right corner of the screen with your mouse, then tap or click on the **Search** charm pointed to in the composite in Fig. 11.14, then:

* Enter **add features** in the text box and tap or click **Settings**.

Fig. 11.14 Adding Features.

- Tap or click **Add features to Windows 8**, then do one of the following:

  - To purchase a product key, tap or click **I want to buy a product key online**. You will be guided through the procedure on screen.

  - If you already have a product key, tap or click **I already have a product key**.

- Enter your product key and tap or click **Next**.

- Accept the license terms and tap or click **Add features**.

If you are running Windows 8, your computer will restart and Windows 8 Pro with **Media Center** will be on it, while if you are running Windows 8 Pro, the computer will restart and **Media Center** will be on it.

Starting Media Center

Windows Media Center

After installing Windows **Media Center**, you will find an additional tile on the **Start** screen, shown here. Tapping or clicking on this tile, starts Windows **Media Center**, as shown in Fig. 11.15 below.

Fig. 11.15 A Media Center Screen.

Now, you might be forgiven if you don't know what to do next, but don't worry because soon you'll come to grips with Windows **Media Center**. Normally the first screen you'll see is that of **Extras** shown at the very top of the screen in Fig. 11.15 on the previous page.

To move from one topic to another, either:

* Swipe upwards and when the required topic is under the focus (a kind of magnifying glass), swipe to the left to bring the options within this topic to the focus.

* Use the keyboard arrow keys; the down-arrow key moves the screen to the next topic, while the right-arrow key moves the screen to the next option within the selected topic.

The available topics are:

Extras	with options to	**extras library** and **explore**
Pictures + Videos	with options to	**picture library**, **play**, **favourites**, **radio** and **search**
Music	with options to	**music library**, **play favourites**, **radio** and **Search**
Movies	with options to	**movie library** and **play dvd**
TV	with options to	**recorded tv** and **live tv setup**
Tasks	with options to	**sync**, **add extender** and **media only**.

All you need to do here is try and see what is offered and soon you will realise what additions to your system are needed to get the most out of **Media Center**.

DVD Playback

The most important function for me is that of being able play a DVD on the laptop. Just insert the DVD into the disc drive and Windows **Media Center** starts playing almost straight away.

Fig. 11.16 Playing a DVD in Media Center.

Help and Support

It is left up to you to explore **Media Center**'s other features listed on the previous page. At any time you can press the **F1** function key to get detailed **Help and Support** from Microsoft on topics such as how to connect your PC to your TV, how to connect your PC to a standard external monitor, keyboard and mouse, and how to stream your media over a home network to a **Media Center** extender.

Depending on your choice, you can watch and record live TV, create slide shows of your photos, listen to songs in your music library, and play CDs and DVDs. You could not ask for more. Have fun!

12

Connectivity & Mobility

Many homes and small offices these days have more than one PC and connecting to a network is a priority so that you can access the Internet from them all, share documents, pictures or music, and print to a single printer. Windows 8 makes this process very much easier than with pre-Windows 7 versions of the Operating System (OS), especially if all the computers are running under the same OS.

Joining a Network

 Although there are many types of networks, such as **Wireless**, **Ethernet**, **HomePNA** and **Powerline**, these days practically everybody uses **Wireless** (WiFi), so only this type of connection is covered here.

To set up a wireless network each computer to be included needs a **Wireless Network Adaptor**. These days all laptops have these built in. With an older desktop PC a network adaptor can be connected to one of its USB ports or installed in an expansion slot.

You will also need a **Wireless Router** to allow access to the Internet and to 'connect' your networked computers. Your Internet Service Provider (ISP) will often offer an ADSL or combination modem/wireless router as part of your Broadband package and some might even come and install it for you. Others might send you the necessary equipment and a CD to make the installation easier for you.

Once you have obtained and installed all this hardware you could, if you so wish, run the **Set up a new network** wizard from the main PC that is attached to the router.

To start the process of networking, use the **Search** charm, as shown in the composite screen dump in Fig. 12.1 below.

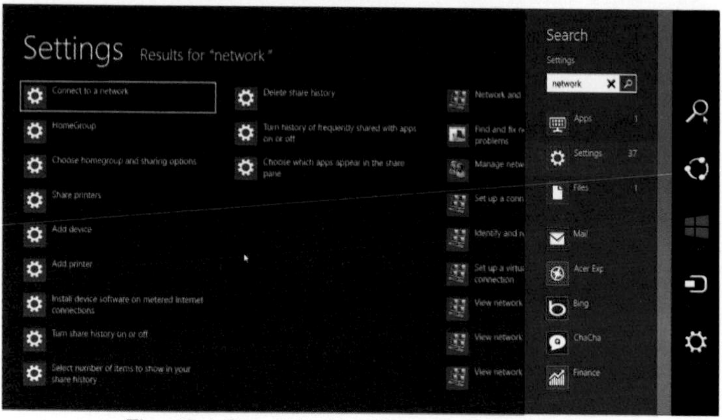

Fig. 12.1 Searching for Network Information.

First type **network** in the search box, then tap or click **Settings**, as shown above. On the left half of the screen you can use a list of options to **Connect to a network**, a **HomeGroup**, **Choose homegroup and sharing options**, **Share printers**, etc. As an example, tap or click on the first item on the list to display a screen similar to that in Fig. 12.2.

The **Connections** screen that opens (Fig. 12.2) displays all the available WiFi networks near you. One of these is your own, if already configured and might already be connected, while the others belong to neighbours and normally require a key to join them. To open this screen in the future, tap or click on the **Network** icon on the right side of the **Taskbar**, 🖳 or ⅷ.

Fig. 12.2 The Connections Screen.

I suggest you have a look at the other **Network** settings in Fig. 12.1, before you try to set up a new connection.

To set up a new connection you need to access the **Network and Sharing Center**, but first you must locate the **Set up a connection or network**

Fig. 12.3 The Set Up a Connection or Network Option.

option which is to be found on the third column of options listed in Fig. 12.1 (partly obscured as it happens) and shown larger here in Fig. 12.3.

Tapping or clicking this option, opens the screen shown in Fig. 12.4 below.

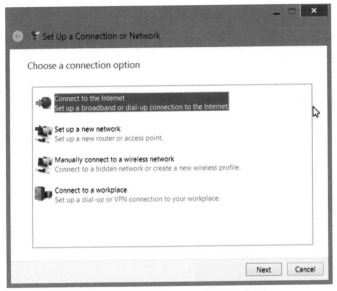

Fig. 12.4 The Network and Sharing Center.

To continue, tap or click the **Set up a new network** – **Set up a new router or access point** option in the window that opens.

You will be stepped through the process of adding other computers and devices to the network. If you need more information here we suggest you look at the options on the first column of Fig. 12.1.

Network Connection

With Windows 8 if a computer has a working network adaptor, the **Network** icon appears in the **Notification** area at the right end of the **Taskbar**.

This icon indicates whether your network adaptor is an **Ethernet** adaptor or a wireless adaptor. With the wireless connection icon the number of bars indicates the signal strength, with 5 being the strongest. When the computer is not connected to a network, an **x** shows on the connection icon, whereas while it is connecting it shows as . When a wireless connection is available, the icon has a starburst.

When you physically connect your computer to a network with an **Ethernet** cable, as is the case here, Windows 8 automatically creates the network connection, but to connect to a wireless network for the first time, you need to make the connection yourself.

Fig. 12.5 Available Wireless Connections.

To demonstrate this, the **Ethernet** cable was removed from my computer. Next, tapping or clicking the available wireless connection icon in the **Notification** area of the **Taskbar** opens a list of available connections, as shown here in Fig. 12.5.

The icon adjacent to each available connection indicates its signal strength. Pretty good here, but not for the bottom one, which happens to be my neighbour's!

If you hover the pointer over an available network connection a screen tip displays information about the connection as shown on the right for one of mine.

Security: WPA2-PSK
Type: 802.11n

Fig. 12.6 Connecting to a Network.

Next, tap or click the connection you want to connect to, and then tap or click the **Connect automatically** box to select it followed by the **Connect** button that appears. If a **WEP** key or **WPA** password is required, you will be prompted to enter it, and then Windows will connect to the selected network.

Wireless Network Security

For very obvious reasons, when you set up a wireless network you should set it up so that only people you choose can access it. There are several wireless network security systems available.

WPA (Wi-Fi Protected Access) encrypts information, checks to make sure that the network security key has not been modified and also authenticates users to help ensure that only authorised people can access the network.

WEP (Wired Equivalent Privacy) is an older network security method that is still available to support older devices. It uses a network security key which encrypts the information sent across your network. However, WEP security is relatively easy to break and is not recommended on its own.

Also 802.1x authentication can help enhance security for 802.11 type wireless networks and wired **Ethernet** networks. It can work with **WPA** or **WEP** keys and uses an authentication server to validate users and provide network access. This is used mainly in company networks.

HomeGroup

The easiest way of getting to **HomeGroup** is via the **Control Panel**. To do this, first activate the **Desktop Internet Explorer** bring up the **Charms** bar, tap or click on the **Settings** charm and select **Control Panel**, as shown in the composite in Fig. 12.7.

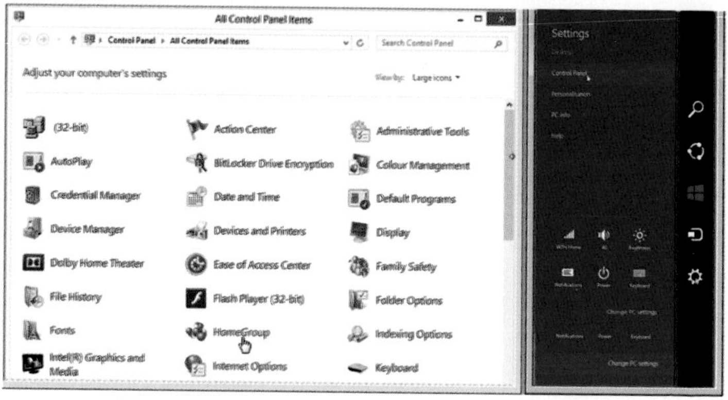

Fig. 12.7 The HomeGroup Control Panel Link.

This feature simplifies the whole network procedure, particularly when the networked PCs are running under Windows 8.

Tapping or clicking the **HomeGroup** link, opens a screen in which you are told that there is a **HomeGroup** available on the network. Using the **Join now** button starts the process.

In the next screen, select what libraries and devices you want to share and tap or click the **Next** button, then tap or click **Next** followed by **Finish** to complete the process.

You have to repeat this procedure to add all your other computers on your home network to the **HomeGroup**. Quite a tedious operation, but it doesn't take long and in the end is well worth the trouble.

> **Note:** It is important to restart the computers for these changes to take effect.

Fig. 12.8 below, displays an example of the connections and sharing permissions of one of my computers.

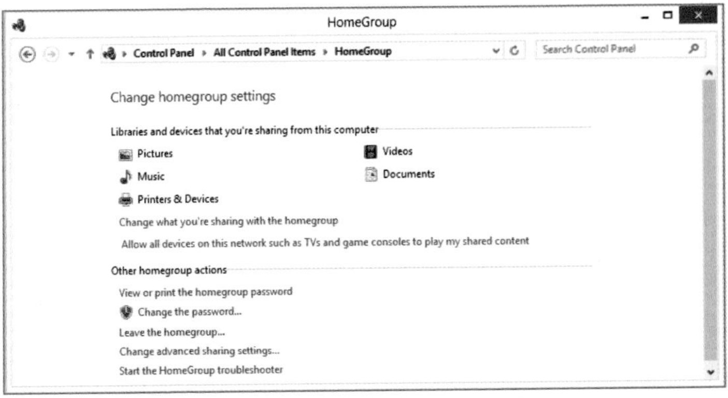

Fig. 12.8 A Computer's HomeGroup Screen.

All your Windows 8 computers in the same **HomeGroup** can share libraries, folders, files, devices and media without ever having to type passwords whenever anything is accessed. You select what you want shared on each computer and as long as it is 'awake' it can be accessed from the other computers in the group with just a few taps or clicks. You can even change what is shared, as shown in Fig. 12. 9.

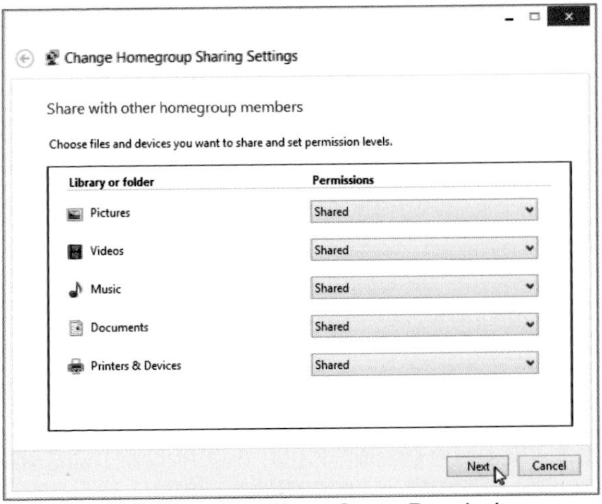

Fig. 12.9 Changing HomeGroup Permissions.

Here you can select what you want to share from a list of your default libraries (**Pictures**, **Videos**, **Music** and **Documents**) and your printers. Check the items you want to share and click on **Next**.

Accessing HomeGroup Computers

Once the **HomeGroup** is created and all your home computers are joined, accessing their shared libraries is very easy. Just open up **File Explorer** and tap or click on **Homegroup** in the **Navigation** pane. In Fig. 12.10, you see the computers that are turned on and are not in sleep mode. The STUDYPC is the computer I am on right now, while NOELSLAPTOP is a computer on the network and I can access all its libraries. Tapping or clicking on a library will open up all the folders and files in it. Very quick, easy and useful.

Fig. 12.10 The Homegroup.

Sharing Printers

To share printers on your network, even if they are not in a **HomeGroup**, so everyone in your household can connect as long as the printers and PCs are switched on, do the following:

*   On the computer that has the printer attached to it, tap or click the **Desktop** tile, then activate the **Charms** bar.

*   Select the **Settings** charm, and tap or click on **Control Panel**.

*   Tap or click the **Devices and Printers** link to open the **Devices and Printers** window, locate the printer attached to the computer, touch and hold or right-click and select **Set as default printer** from the displayed drop-down menu.

*   For the same printer, touch and hold or right-click and select **Printer properties** from the displayed drop-down menu to open the **Properties** dialogue box.

- Tap or click the **Sharing** tab, and tap or click the [⚙ Change Sharing Options] button and tap or click the **Share this printer** box to select it, then press **OK** to approve the options and close the **Properties** dialogue box..

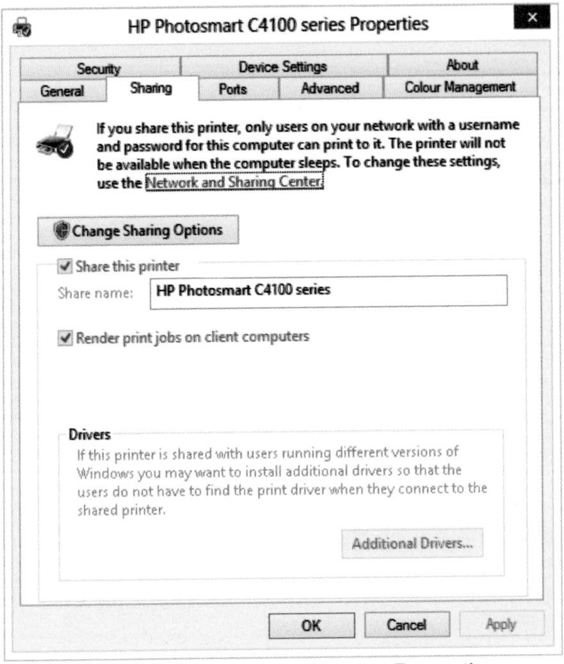

Fig. 12.11 The Printer's Sharing Properties.

Before you can use a shared printer from your other Windows 8 PCs on the network, you have to add it to the list of available printers on each of the PCs, by doing the following:

- Open the **Devices and Printers** window again as described on the previous page and click the [Add a printer] button.

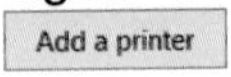

- Select the option to **Add a printer**, and pick your printer from the list, as shown in Fig. 12.12 on the next page.

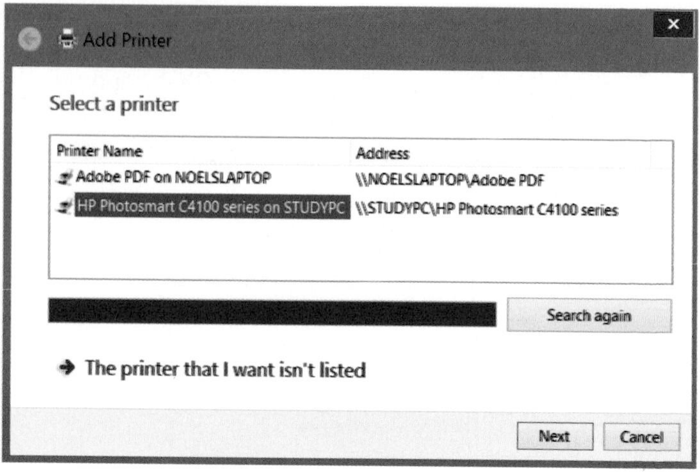

Add Printer   ✕

Select a printer

Printer Name	Address
Adobe PDF on NOELSLAPTOP	\\NOELSLAPTOP\Adobe PDF
HP Photosmart C4100 series on STUDYPC	\\STUDYPC\HP Photosmart C4100 series

[   ]   Search again

➡ The printer that I want isn't listed

                                          Next   Cancel

Fig. 12.12 Available Networked Printers.

- Click **Next**, and wait for the printer driver to be located and loaded. When this is done you can then print a test page to make sure everything works.

Now any computer on the network can select the printer and use it just as if it were directly connected. To illustrate this Fig. 12.13 below shows part of the **Devices and Printers** window from a networked laptop.

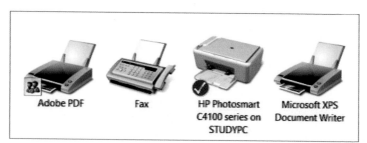

Adobe PDF   Fax   HP Photosmart   Microsoft XPS
                        C4100 series on   Document Writer
                        STUDYPC

Fig. 12.13 Accessing a Shared Printer over the Network.

Using the Network

Once all the sharing and permissions have been sorted out you can access the other computers and printers in your network from the **File Explorer** window. As shown in Fig. 12.14 they are listed in the **Homegroup** item on the **Navigation** pane.

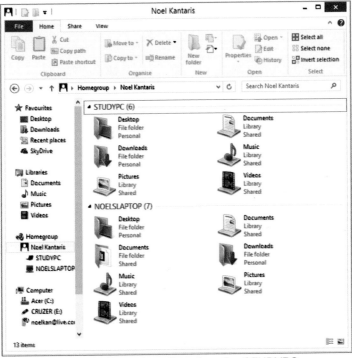

Fig. 12.14 Network as Seen from the STUDYPC.

The above example shows how I can access my laptop from my STUDYPC. I can open and move files between them and even open and stream music and videos. In other words we can start a video located on the desktop and have it play on the laptop. These features are well worth the effort involved.

Adding a Windows 7 PC to the Network

To add a PC running Windows 7 to the established wireless network, do the following:

- On the PC running Windows 7, use the **Start**, **Control Panel** option to open the **Control Panel**, then find and click on the **Network and Sharing Center** to open the screen shown in Fig. 12.15.

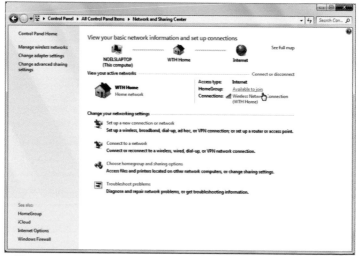

Fig. 12.15 The Network and Sharing Screen on a Windows 7 PC.

- Click the **Available to Join** link, pointed to in Fig. 12.15, to open a further screen with links to information about **HomeGroups** and **Sharing**. On such a screen, click the **Join now** button to open the first Wizard screen shown in Fig. 12.16 on the next page.

- Select on this screen what you want to share and click **Next** to open the second Wizard screen, shown in Fig 12.17, also shown on the next page. On this screen you are asked to enter the network password. If you don't know this password, click the **Where can I find the homegroup password** link to open a **Help** screen telling you how to find it. I have included this information at the bottom of Fig. 12.17.

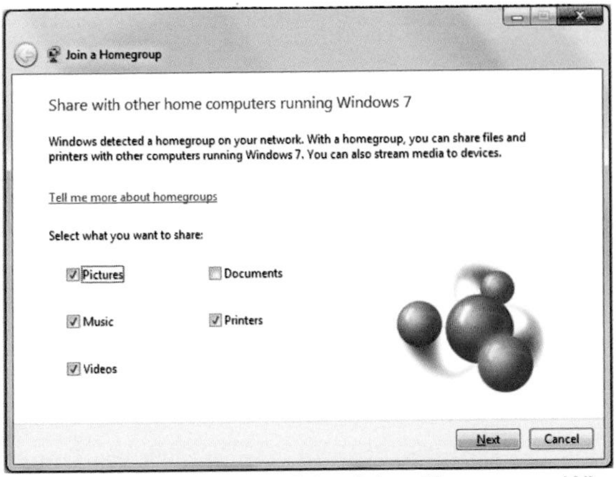

Fig. 12.16 The First Screen of the Join a Homegroup Wizard.

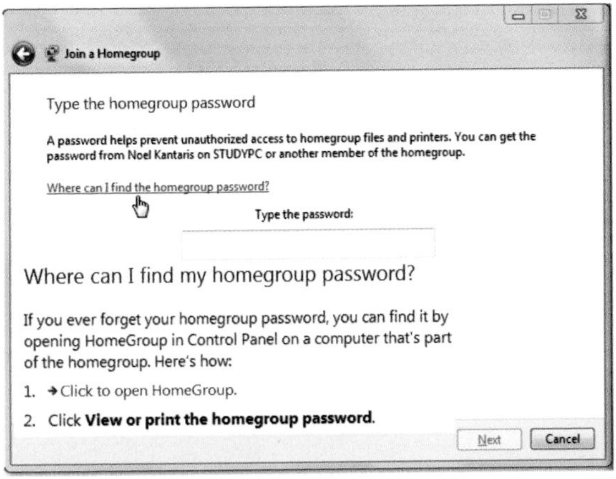

Fig. 12.17 The Second Screen of the Join a Homegroup Wizard.

- Next, type the password into the box of the above screen and click **Next**, which opens the final Wizard screen informing you that you have succeeded in joining the **Homegroup**.

It might be a good idea if you tried to print a word processed page from your Windows 7 PC to see if all is as it should be, remembering that the PC which is connected to the printer should be switched on.

Mobility

By mobility I am referring here to computer mobility, not your ability to get around! One of the nice things about using Windows 8 on a **mobile** notebook or netbook PC is that the most important configuration options are consolidated into a single utility, the **Windows Mobility Center**. This is where you should go when you want to control how your mobile PC works.

Windows Mobility Center

To launch the **Mobility Center**, tap or click the **Desktop** tile in the **Start** screen, then activate the **Charms** bar. Next, tap or click the **Settings** charm, and select **Control Panel**.

At nearly the very end of the **Control Panel** list, you will find the **Windows Mobility Center** link shown here. Tapping or clicking on this link, opens a window like the one in Fig. 12.18 below.

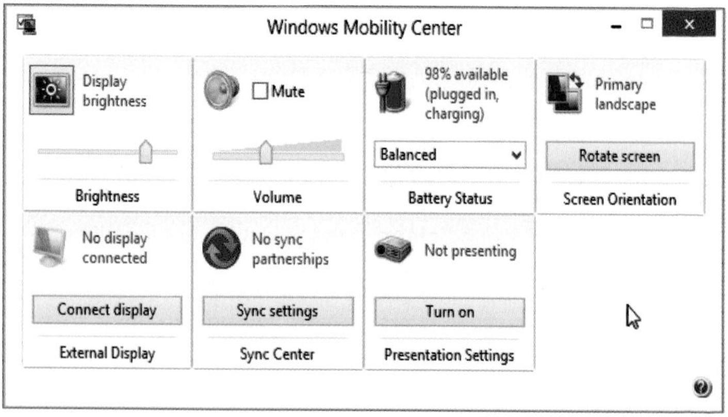

Fig. 12.18 Windows Mobility Center for a Laptop.

The **Mobility Center** includes panels for the most common laptop settings. These are:

Brightness

 Display brightness

A slider temporarily adjusts the display brightness. If you hover the mouse over the display icon it turns into a button which opens the **Power Options** window, where you can change the brightness level on your current power plan.

Volume

 ☐ Mute

Adjusts the volume level of your computer's sound and lets you mute it. Tap or click the speaker graphic to open the **Sound** dialogue box where you can adjust all the audio settings on your laptop.

Battery Status

Displays the current charge status of your computer's battery and lets you change the power plan. Tap or click the battery graphic, to open the **Power Options** window where you can edit the power plans and create your own custom power plans, as discussed in the next section.

Screen Orientation

  Primary landscape

Displays the orientation of your screen. Tap or click the screen graphic to open the **Screen Resolution** panel , where you can change the appearance of your display.

External Display

No display connected

Lets you connect your laptop to an external monitor or projector. Tap or click the display graphic to open the **Screen Resolution** window where you can change the resolution and orientation of both your internal and external displays.

Tap or click the **Connect display** button to open the options available for projecting to a secondary screen.

Sync Center

No sync partnerships

Lets you check the results of your recent synchronisation activity if you've set up your computer to sync files with a network server.

All in all this is a very useful facility for mobile users. Some notebook manufacturers might include their own panels.

Note: The **Mobility Center** by default, is only available on laptops, netbooks, and tablet PCs. It is not available on desktop computers unless it is enabled.

Power Plans

If you are worried when using a laptop away from the mains about how much power it is using, then read on as even the best batteries seem to run low far too quickly!

As well as the **Battery Status** tile in the **Mobility Center**, the battery meter in the **Notification** area of the **Taskbar** shows you the state of your laptop's battery. If you hover over it, the % charge appears. If you tap it or click it, a pop-up like that in Fig. 12.19 opens showing what power plan is active.

Fig. 12.19.

The Windows 8 **Power Plans** cater for three main power designs that can help you save energy, maximise system performance, or achieve a balance between the two. To see the default power plans, tap or click the **More power options** link in the above pop-up to open the **Power Options** window shown in Fig. 12.20 on the next page.

You can also open the **Power Options** window from the **Battery Status** tile in the **Mobility Center**, or by tapping or clicking the **Power Options** link in the **Control Panel**.

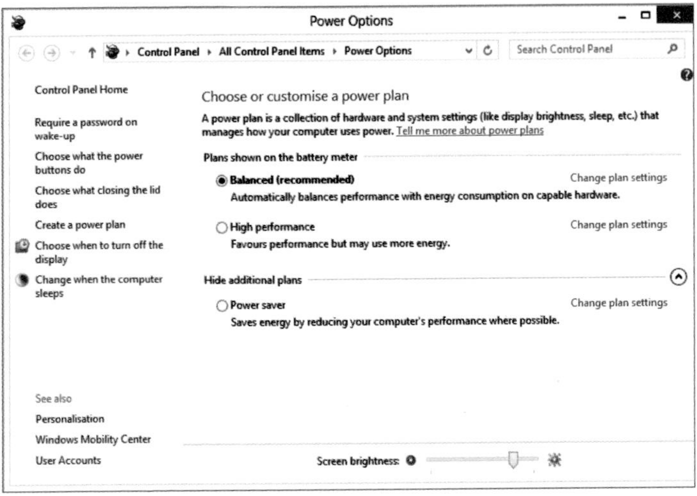

Fig. 12.20 The Power Options Window.

The three default **Power Plans** are:

Balanced – Giving good performance when it is needed, but saving power during periods of inactivity.

High performance – Giving maximum brightness and performance, but using far more power, making it rather unhelpful to mobile users unless they are plugged in to the mains.

Power saver – Saves power by reducing screen brightness and system performance. This can be useful if you are ever 'caught out'.

Which plan to use? For most people much of the time the default **Balanced** plan is a good compromise between battery life and performance. Many people will never change it from the recommended option.

When you are away from home and operating on batteries the **Power saver** plan will probably give you a few more minutes of battery life, but do remember to reduce display brightness as this uses more power than any other part of a computer. Also disconnect devices that you are not actually using, such as USB devices which use power just by being connected.

You should only really use the **High performance** plan when you are connected to mains power and have a full battery charge.

These three power plans should meet your needs most of the time, but if you want to build your own, then you can use one of the default power plans as a starting point. All of them can be adapted by clicking on their **Change plan settings** link in the **Power Options** window. The main settings in the **Edit Plan Settings** windows that open are when to **Turn off the display**, and when to **Put the computer to sleep**. But the **Change advanced power settings** link gives you almost absolute control over everything, as shown in Fig. 12.21.

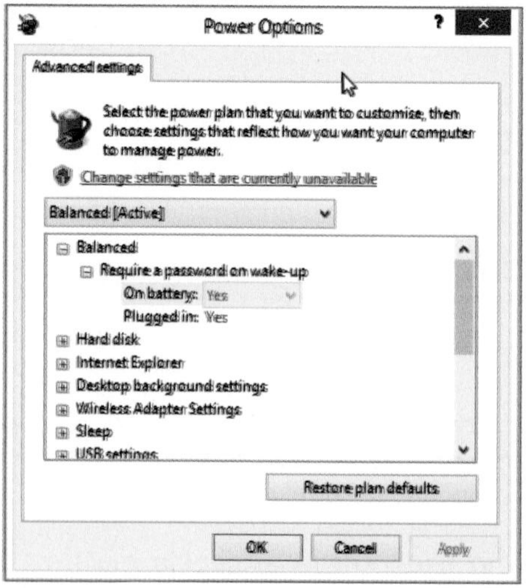

Fig. 12.21 Changing Advanced Power Settings.

You do have lots of option to examine and think about of their effect, so spending some time here might be worthwhile.

13

Looking After Your PC

Windows 8 comes equipped with a full range of utilities for you to easily maintain your PC's health and well being. You can access some of these tools by tapping or clicking the **Desktop** tile in the **Start** menu, selecting the **Settings Charm** from the **Charms** bar, then tapping or clicking the **PC info** option listed under **Settings** and pointed to in Fig. 13.1. This opens the **System Information** screen shown in Fig. 13.2.

Fig. 13.1 Settings Options.

View basic information about your computer

Control Panel Home

Device Manager
Remote settings
System protection
Advanced system settings

Windows edition

Windows 8 Pro with Media Center

© 2012 Microsoft Corporation. All rights reserved.

Windows®8

System

Rating:	**5.5** Windows Experience Index
Processor:	Intel(R) Core(TM) i7-3517U CPU @ 1.90GHz 1.90 GHz
Installed memory (RAM):	4.00 GB (3.82 GB usable)
System type:	64-bit Operating System, x64-based processor
Pen and Touch:	Full Windows Touch Support with 10 Touch Points

Computer name, domain and workgroup settings

Computer name:	StudyPC	Change settings
Full computer name:	StudyPC	
Computer description:		
Workgroup:	WORKGROUP	

See also

Action Center
Windows Update
Performance Information and Tools

Windows activation

Fig. 13.2 System Information Screen.

This is the easiest to take a first look at – it displays such things as your Operating System, System Summary, Hardware Resources, etc. However, each computer is bound to be different, so don't expect to see the same information, but what is important here are the links at the left of the screen which deal with prevention of system problems.

Problem Prevention

Windows 8 has strong protection against **System** corruption:

- System Protection
- System Restore
- Automatic Update

Each of these will be discussed separately.

System Protection

Windows applications sometimes can, and do, overwrite important **System** files. Windows 8 protects your **System** files by automatically saving them at regular intervals, but you must check the settings and if necessary change them.

The first setting to be checked is the **System Protection**. To do this, tap or click the **System protection** link at the top-left corner in Fig. 13.2 to open the tabbed dialogue box shown in Fig. 13.3.

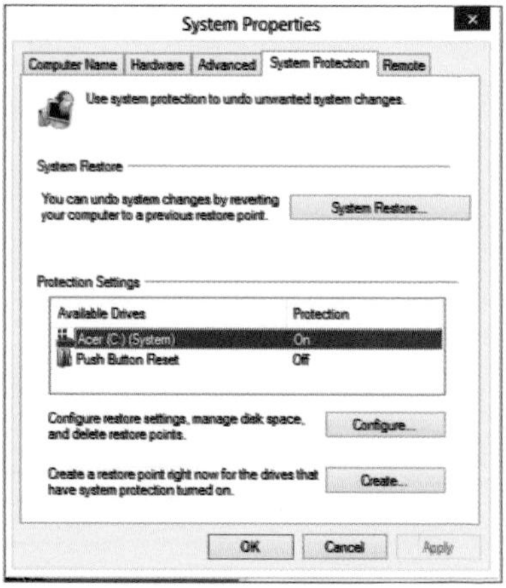

Fig. 13.3 System Protection Tab.

With the **System Protection** tab selected, check that the C: drive (the one that Windows 8 is installed on), under **Protection Settings** in Fig. 13.3, is **On**.

If not, select the option, then tap or click the **Configure** button. This displays the dialogue box shown in Fig. 13.4.

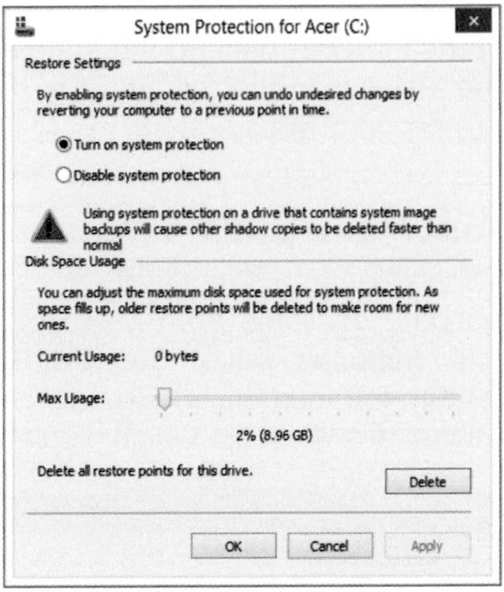

Next, tap or click the **Turn on system protection** radio button to select it and move the slider next to **Max Usage** to, say, 2% to indicate the maximum disc space to be used for system protection, then tap or click **Apply**, followed by **OK**.

Fig. 13.4 System Protection.

This returns you to the dialogue box of Fig. 13.3 where you should tap or click the **Create** button to create a restore point right now. On the dialogue box that opens, give the restore point a descriptive name, and tap or click **Create**.

In the future, you can undo system changes by reverting your PC to the state it was when you created the restore point. This is done by activating the **System Restore** button in Fig. 13.3 which starts the **System Restore** Wizard.

Tapping or clicking **Next** displays a dialogue box similar to that shown in Fig. 13.5.

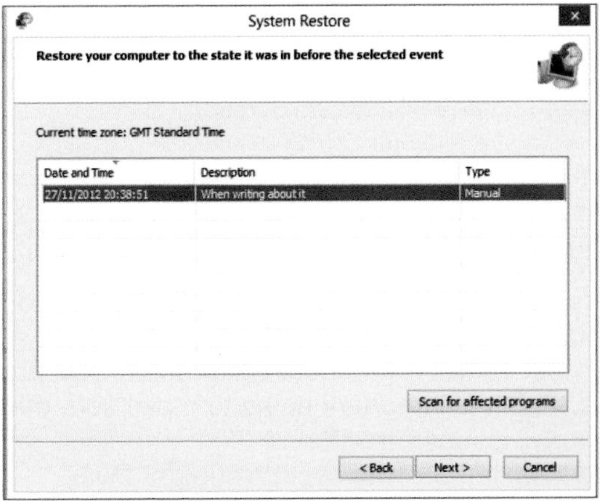

Fig. 13.5 System Restore Points.

Restore points are created automatically by the system every time you install or uninstall a program. This is a precaution just in case a newly installed program creates problems, so you can revert back to the state the computer was in prior to the installation that caused the problem. This is an excellent protection of your system.

Automatic Update

Windows can automatically update any **System** files as they become available from Microsoft's Web site. To make sure this happens, click the **Windows Update** link at the bottom-left corner in Fig. 13.2. This will connect you to Microsoft's Web site which displays the screen in Fig. 13.6.

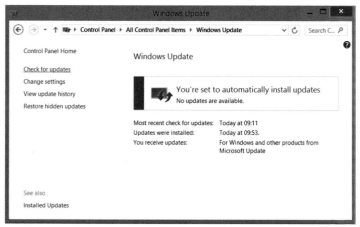

Fig. 13.6 Windows Update Screen.

As you can see from the above screen, the system has been set to automatically install updates. If that is not the case, you can use the **Change settings** link to do so. This is important.

The **Change settings** link displays a window in which you can choose to **Install updates automatically**, as shown in Fig. 13.7 on the next page. This should guarantee you are always up to date, which is important so as to make sure that as possible security issues are found and corrected by Microsoft they are installed on your system straight away.

Change settings — □ ✕

← → ⌄ ↑ 📁 « All Control Panel Items ▸ Windows Update ▸ Change settings   ⌄ ♻   Search C... 🔎

Choose your Windows Update settings

When your PC is online, Windows can automatically check for important updates and install them using these settings. When new updates are available, you can also choose to install them when you shut down your PC.

Important updates

🛡 | Install updates automatically (recommended)   ⌄ |

Updates will be automatically downloaded in the background when your PC is not on a metered Internet connection.

Updates will be automatically installed during the maintenance window.

Recommended updates

☑ Give me recommended updates the same way I receive important updates

Microsoft Update

☑ Give me updates for other Microsoft products when I update Windows

Note: Windows Update might update itself automatically first when checking for other updates. Read our privacy statement online.

🛡 OK   Cancel

Fig. 13.7 Windows Update Settings Screen.

If you have to change the settings to the recommended one, then tap or click the **Check for updates** link at the top-left corner in Fig. 13.6, to get a list of updates for your system.

With the recommended settings all critical updates will be downloaded and installed automatically while non-critical ones will display a pop-up similar to the one shown here.

System and Security

To examine the other options in the Windows **System and Security center**, tap or click the **Desktop** tile on the **Start** screen, then use the **Settings** charm and select **Control Panel**. Next, choose to **View by: Category**, and click the **System and Security** icon, shown here, to display the window shown in Fig. 13.8 overleaf.

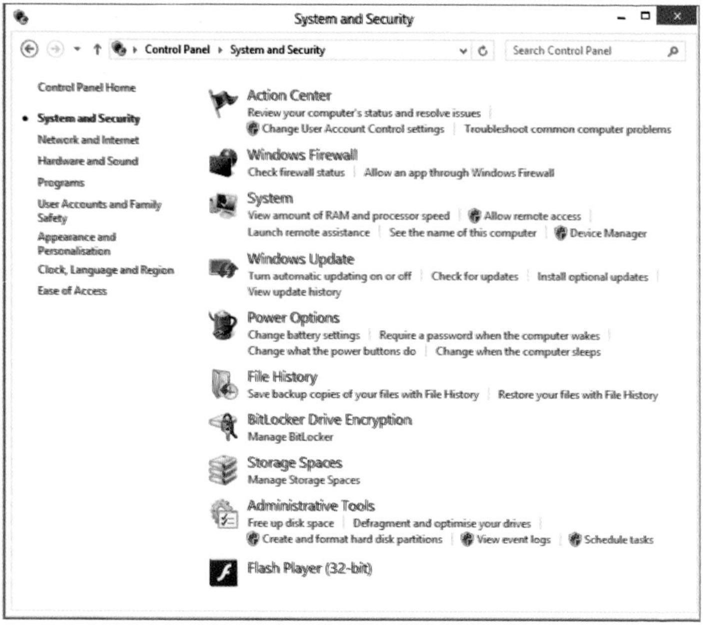

Fig. 13.8 The Windows System and Security Screen.

Action Center

The **Action Center** looks after message alerts from key Windows security and maintenance features. When Windows requires your attention, the **Action Center** icon appears in the **Taskbar**. Tapping or clicking this icon opens a pop-up box (Fig. 13.9) which lists the problems and gives suggested fixes for them. You can then tap or click a solution to solve a problem.

Fig. 13.9 A Pop-up Alert Box.

You can also open the **Action Center** itself to fine-tune your requirements by clicking the **Action Center** link in Fig. 13.8 above.

Important items are labelled in red, to indicate that they are significant and should be addressed straight away. In the example in Fig. 13.9 there was no **Firewall** open, but just clicking the **View firewall options** button, lets you cure the problem instantly. Yellow items are suggested tasks, such as recommended maintenance, that you should consider doing.

Windows Firewall

For your PC to be secure, make sure that the Windows **Firewall** is switched on. Tapping or clicking the **Check firewall status** link, displays the screen shown in Fig. 13.10.

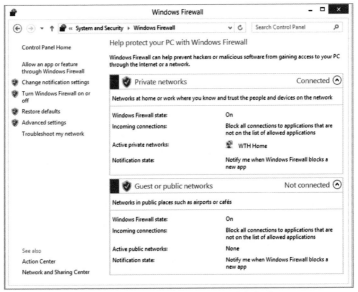

Fig. 13.10 The Windows Firewall Window.

A **Firewall** is a software security system that sits between your computer and the outside world and is used to set restrictions on what information is passed to and from the Internet. In other words it protects you from uninvited access.

If your **Firewall** is turned off, or you do not have up-to-date virus protection, the **Action Center** will flag an error by placing the 🔖 icon in the **Notification** area of the **Taskbar**.

Hard Disc Management

There are two Apps in Windows 8 to help you keep your hard disc in good condition: **Disk Clean-up**, which removes unnecessary files from your hard disc and frees up space, and **Defragment and Optimise Drives** which optimises your hard discs by rearranging their data to eliminate unused spaces, which speeds up access to your hard discs.

Disk Clean-up

To start **Disk Clean-up**, tap or click the **Desktop** tile on the **Start** screen, then activate the **Charms** bar, select the **Search** charm and type **disk** in the search box, as shown in the composite in Fig. 13.11.

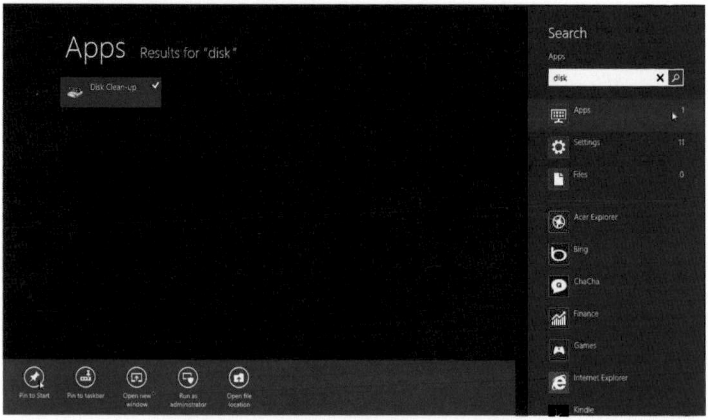

Fig. 13.11 The Disk Clean-up App.

Since you should use this App at least once a week, it might be a good idea to place a tile of it on the **Start** screen. To do this, right-click it to open the **Tools** bar at the bottom of the screen, then tap or click the **Pin to Start** button.

Note: If you are a tablet user, you'll find that touching and holding does not emulate right-clicking in this instance – it simply starts the App.

Tapping or clicking the **Disk Clean-up** tile opens the **Drive Selection** box shown in Fig. 13.12.

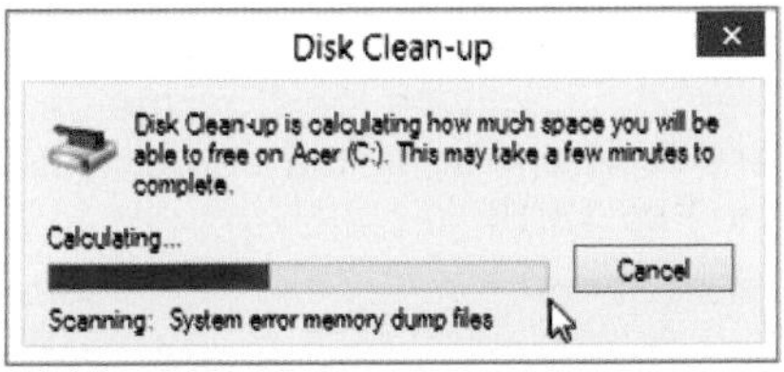

Fig. 13.12 Selecting Drive.

As my computer has only one hard disc, the **Disk Clean-up** starts immediately. If your system has more than one hard disc, then you'll be given the opportunity to select which disc you want to operate on before the **Disk Clean-up** scans the drive. It then lists temporary files, Internet cache files, and other files that you can safely delete, as shown in Fig. 13.13.

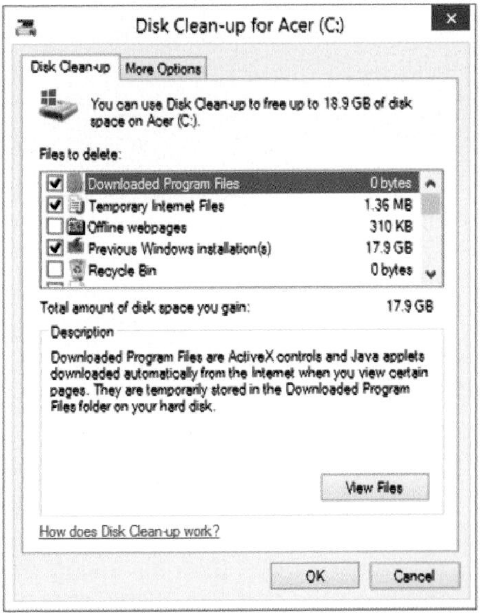

Fig. 13.13 Files Found that can be Cleaned Up.

As you can see, on my setup, I could free some considerable disc space by deleting all the files selected (the longer you use your PC the larger the files that could be deleted), and especially by deleting the **Previous Windows Installation(s)** as well – I did upgrade from Windows 8 to Windows 8 Pro.

Defragmenting Hard Discs

To start **Disk Defragmenter**, tap or click the **Desktop** tile on the **Start** screen, then activate the **Charms** bar, select the **Search** charm and type **defrag** in the search box, as shown in the composite in Fig. 13.14.

Fig. 13.14 Finding and Creating a Disk Defragmenting App.

Just as with **Disk Clean-up**, you could create a tile on the **Start** screen by right-clicking the App and tapping or clicking the **Pin to Start** button on the **Toolbar** that displays at the bottom of the screen.

The **Disk Defragmenter** optimises your hard discs by rearranging their data to eliminate unused spaces, which speeds up access by all Windows and other program operations. By default it is set to run automatically every week, but you can change this by using the **Run as administrator** tool pointed to in Fig. 13.14 above. This opens the screen in Fig. 13.15 shown on the next page.

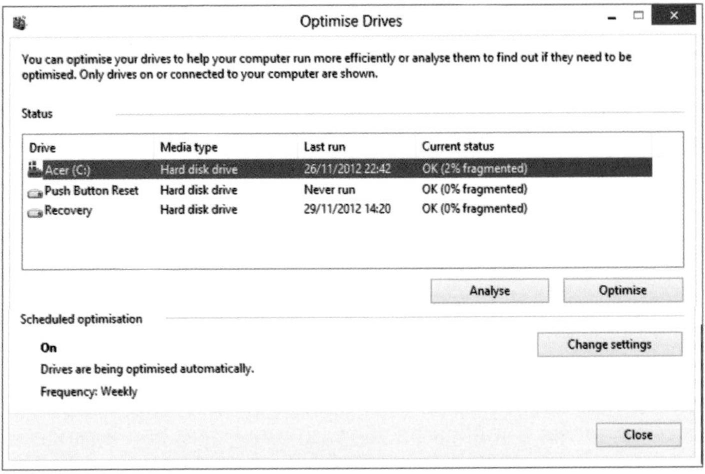

Fig. 13.15 The Optimise Drives Screen.

Tapping or clicking the **Change settings** button under the **Scheduled optimisation** section, displays the screen in Fig. 13.16.

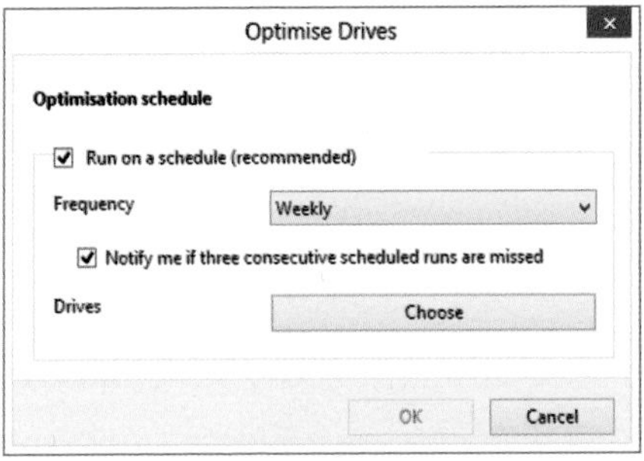

Fig. 13.16 Optimisation Schedule and Drive Selection.

You can also analyse and defragment your discs and drives manually. These days you don't even need to close running Apps or programs before starting the **Disk Defragmenter**.

If the percentage of fragmentation on the disc is high, you should defragment the disc. You can defragment a drive in the background by minimising the window to the **Taskbar** and carry on with your work as normal. This is extremely useful, as defragmenting a large disc can take well over half an hour, but depends on how full the disc is. The fuller the disc, the longer the defragmentation process.

Backing up your Data

Anyone can lose files by either accidentally deleting or replacing them, a virus attack, or a software or hardware failure, such as a complete hard disc failure. With Windows, you can use **System Restore** to recover your system files, you can reinstall your programs, but what about your precious data files, cherished pictures and videos of your family? To protect these, you should regularly create backups, or set of copies of your data files, stored in a different location.

Too many people don't think about backing up their data until it has already been lost! Please don't let this happen to you. Windows 8 makes backing up easy, and has a range of features to seamlessly protect your data and system setup.

Data Backup

Windows 8 allows you to back up your data files and recover them later. To find the application that does this, activate the **Charms** bar and type **data backup** in the **Search** box and tap or click the **Settings** entry, as shown in Fig. 13.17

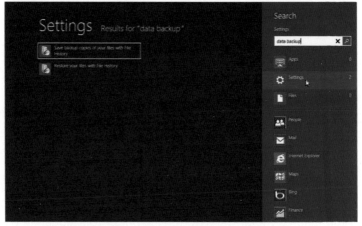

Fig. 13.17 Locating File History Applications.

You need to attach an external USB drive to your computer so that saved files can be copied to it. Having done this, tap or click the **Save backup copies of your files with File History**, to open the screen in Fig. 13.18 below.

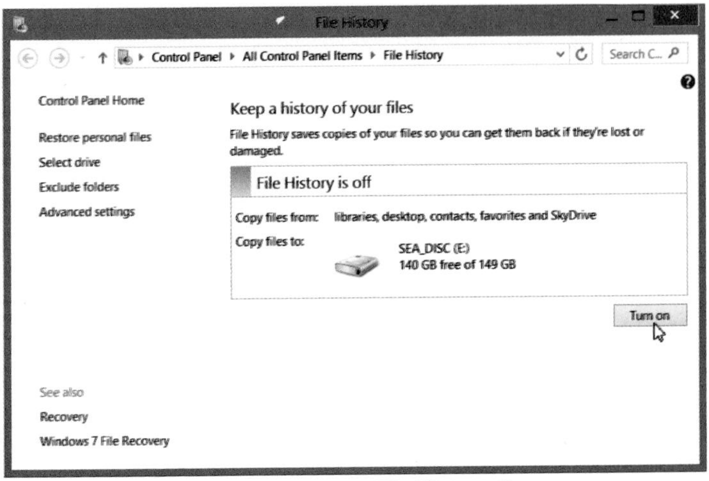

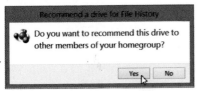

Fig. 13.18 Turning File History On.

The first thing to do here is to tap or click the **Turn on** button so that **File History** is turned on, which displays the suggestion box in Fig. 13.19 below.

Fig. 13.19 Suggestion Box.

Obviously, it might be a good idea to accept the suggestion, but that is up to you. What will be saved are all the **Libraries**, the **Desktop**, all your **Contacts**, **Favourites** and all the files on your **SkyDrive**.

Do look at the options listed on the left-top corner of the display in Fig. 13.18. Having started the process, be patient, especially if this is the first time you are saving your files. You'll know it is done when the date of the last save appears under the image of the external disc in Fig. 13.18.

Subsequent Backups

Once you create the initial backup, you really never have to think about backing up your files again since Windows will regularly do this for you according to the schedule you set.

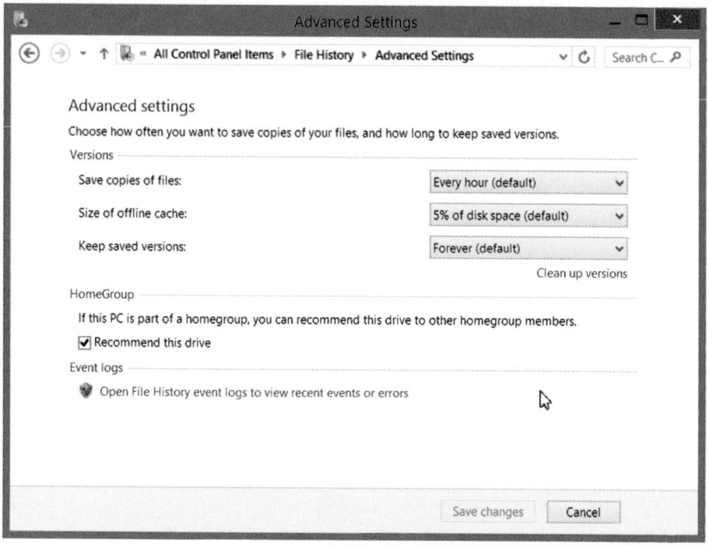

Fig. 13.20 The Advanced Settings Screen.

Perhaps saving your files every hour might be a bit disruptive, so you might want to change that option. You can also choose to delete older backups to save disc space.

Restoring from Backups

Restoring files and folders from your backups is very easy. There can be several backups (depending on the frequency of backing up your data in **Advanced Settings**), from which to make a choice. You do this by selecting the second option of the search results, in Fig. 13.17 also shown here. Tapping or clicking this option, immediately displays a screen similar to that in Fig. 13.21 on the next page.

Fig. 13.21 Files to be Restored.

From here you can restore your files by selecting which backup to use. Tapping or clicking the green circular arrow will restore the latest backup, but you can also select whether you want to restore files from an older backup by using the left-pointing arrow or return to more recent backups by using the right-pointing arrow.

You would normally pick to restore your selection to their original location, unless you want them somewhere else, in which case right-click the green button and select from the drop-down menu, as shown here.

If you need to make an 'image backup' of your whole drive, meaning everything on your hard drive, Windows **System** files, all your additional installed programs and all your data, then you have to resort to programs specifically design for the purpose. A quick search on the Internet should reveal a host of such programs, but make quite sure that the one you choose is compatible with Windows 8 (many are not)!

A system image is a copy of the drive required for Windows to run, and can be used to restore your computer if the hard drive breaks down. However, some programs cannot restore individual files from a system image backup, only the full image, others can, so it's up to you which to choose to serve your needs!

A system image is a particularly good idea just after you have installed Windows 8 and have all your drivers and working programs set up and running. Your PC will be uncluttered and will be running at its fastest then. If disaster strikes, that is a good place to rapidly return to and restore your system. All you will have to do then is download updates and restore your data files.

Windows Defender

Windows **Defender** is free anti-spyware software that can be downloaded from:

www.windowsdefender.com

Windows **Defender** helps protect your computer against spyware and other potentially dangerous software being installed on your computer when you are connected to the Internet. It offers two ways to help keep infections at bay:

- In real-time, it alerts you when spyware attempts to install itself on your computer, tries to run on it, or attempts to change Windows settings.

- At any time, you can scan for spyware that might be installed on your computer, having bypassed Windows **Defender**, and automatically remove them and the problems they may cause.

To open Windows **Defender**, action the **Charms** bar, select **Settings**, then **Control Panel**. Nearly at the bottom of the displayed list of options (viewed in **Large icons**), tap or click the option shown here.

This action opens a screen similar to that shown in Fig. 13.22, provided the **Defender** is turned on. If it is not, you may get a message asking you to do so.

Fig. 13.22 The Defender's PC Status Screen.

As you can see, in my case the **Defender** is turned on and the **PC Status** is **Protected**. However, the first time the **Defender** is opened, you will get a window in which you'll be asked to **Check for new definitions**. With Windows **Defender**, it is very important to have up-to-date 'definitions', or files listing potential software threats. Once it is switched on the program will work with Windows **Update** to automatically install new definitions and keep them up to date.

With Windows **Defender** you can run three types of scan of your computer:

- **Quick** which checks the most likely places on your hard disc that spyware will be located. This is the default type and starts when you action **Scan now**.

- **Full** which checks all your files and all currently running programs, but will seriously slow down your computer while it is taking place.

- **Custom** which allows you to select which partition, hard drive or attached drives to scan.

Microsoft recommends that you **Turn on real-time protection** which you can set in the screen of the **Settings** tab. You can, of course, run a full scan if you think that your computer is infected.

The real-time spyware protection alerts you when spyware or other potentially unwanted software tries to install itself, or run, on your PC. It also notifies you when Apps try to change important settings.

Windows **Defender** operates under three alert levels and depending on the level, it informs you or acts as follows:

- If the alert level is 'severe' or 'high', for example the software tries to change settings which will damage your PC, or tries to collect information without your knowledge, then Windows **Defender** will remove such software automatically.

- If the alert level is 'medium', for example the software tries to affect your privacy or change settings on your PC after notifying you and asking your permission, then you will be offered a choice to either allow or block such software. You should consider blocking it, if you don't recognise or trust the originator of this software.

- If the alert level is 'low', for example the software might try to collect information about you or your PC, after asking permission to do so, then you should only consider blocking if you don't recognise or trust the originator of the software.

For more in-depth information, perhaps you should look at Windows **Defender Help**, accessed by clicking the ❷ button in Fig. 13.22.

User Account Control

User Account Control (UAC), is a very important Windows 8 security feature which helps to prevent unauthorised changes to your computer by programs, viruses or other users through a network.

When an App (or program) tries to make system changes such as: the installation of new software, modifications of **System** files and folders, or modifications which affect other users, **UAC** prompts you to ask for permission, as in Fig. 13.23.

Fig. 13.23 A User Account Control Prompt.

If you click **No** the change is not performed. If you click **Yes** you give the application administrative permissions to make **System** changes during the current session.

The easiest way to open **User Account Control** is to action the **Charms** bar, select **Search**, type **uca** in the **Search** box, tap or click the **Settings** option and select the Change User Account Control settings option. Alternatively, you can find it with the **Control Panel**, **Action Center**, **Change User Account Control settings** sequence.

The **UAC** window that opens has a slider as shown in Fig. 13.24 on the next page. You can drag this slider to change your **UAC** settings. By default, as shown, it is set to notify you only when programs try to make changes to your computer.

This is the best setting to use. It gives good protection and only bothers you when you try to open an old program, or when something dangerous is about to happen.

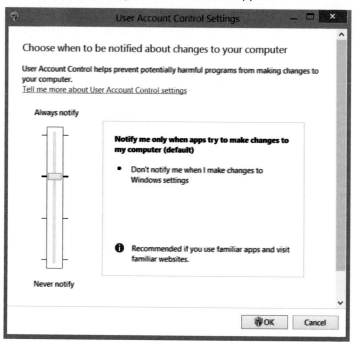

Fig. 13.24 The Default Windows 8 UAC Settings.

When you first open the **UAC** window the handle of the slider is not visible. To make it so, you must first double-tap or double-click between the two black lines (the default position of the slider). The four **UAC** levels to choose from are:

1. Always notify me when – (a) Apps try to install software or make changes to my computer, (b) I make changes to Windows settings. This is the most secure setting but very annoying. You are always notified before any changes are made. The **UAC** prompt opens and your **Desktop** background is dimmed. You cannot use your computer until you choose **Yes** or **No**. I don't recommend this setting!

2. Notify me only when apps try to make changes to my computer (default) – On this setting, the computer only prompts you before programs make changes that require administrative permissions. This level is less annoying as it doesn't stop you making changes to the system, but only shows prompts if an application wants to make changes. The **Desktop** is still dimmed and you must choose **Yes** or **No** before you can do anything else on your computer. This is the best setting to use.

3. Notify me only when apps try to make changes to my computer (do not dim my desktop) – Identical to 2 above except that the **Desktop** is not dimmed. This level is less secure as it is easier for malicious programs to simulate keystrokes or mouse moves which interfere with the **UAC** prompt.

4. Never notify when – Apps try to install software or make changes to my computer or I make changes to Windows settings. This level of the **UAC** doesn't offer any protection and is not recommended. It makes it much easier for rogue programs to infect your computer and even take control of it.

Note: Whatever else you do with the **UAC** level settings, make sure you don't use the 'never notify' setting or you will regret it one day!

14

Accessibility

The Ease of Access Center

If you have problems using a standard computer Windows 8 has several features that may be of help.

 The **Ease of Access Center** lets you change settings to make your PC more accessible if you have visual or hearing difficulties, suffer pain in your hands or arms and/or have other reasoning and cognitive issues.

You can open the **Ease of Access Center** by using the **Settings** charm, then selecting **Control Panel** and tapping or clicking the **Ease of Access Center**, as shown in the composite screen dump in Fig. 14.1.

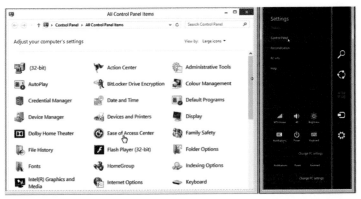

Fig. 14.1 The Ease of Access Center Entry in the Control Panel.

However, by far the easiest way to open the **Ease of Access Center**, if you have a keyboard, is by using the ⊞+U keyboard shortcut (where ⊞ is the Windows key on your keyboard).

Both methods open the screen shown in Fig. 14.2 below.

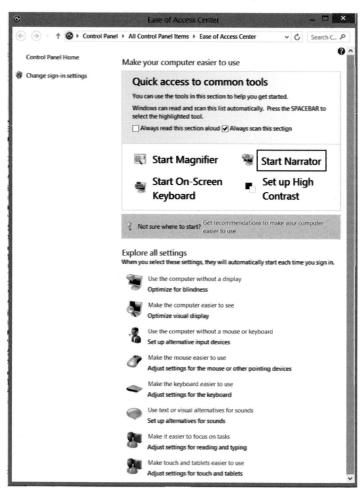

Fig. 14.2 The Ease of Access Center Screen.

The **Ease of Access Center** includes a quick access panel at the top with a highlight rotating through the four most common tools; **Start Magnifier**, **Start Narrator**, **Start On-Screen Keyboard**, and **Set up High Contrast**. A voice, the Narrator, also tells you what option is selected.

Pressing the **Spacebar** on a highlighted option will start that option. If the Narrator annoys you, click the **Always read this section aloud** box to remove the tick mark from it. While you are doing this, you could also remove the tick mark from the **Always scan this section** box, to stop the focus from rotating between the four entries.

The 💡 **Get recommendations to make your computer easier to use** link opens a five-stage questionnaire, the first screen of which is shown in Fig. 14.3 below.

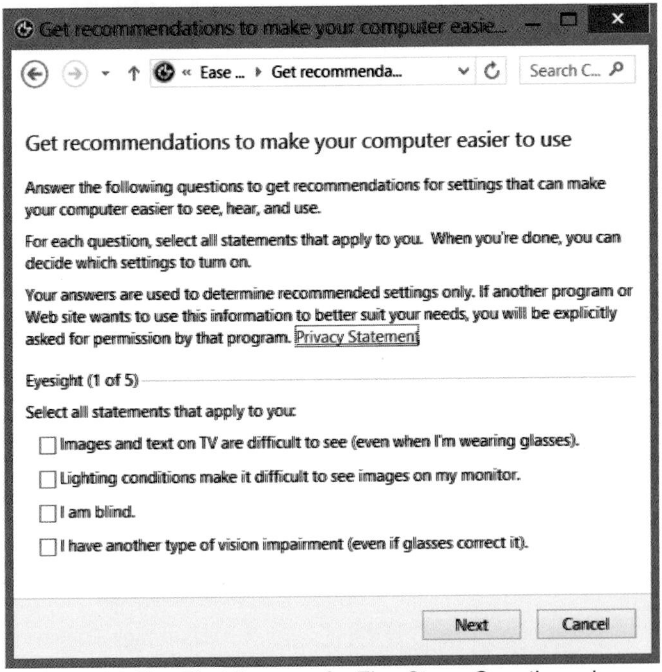

Fig. 14.3 The First Screen of a Five Stage Questionnaire.

Depending on your answers to questions about performing routine tasks, such as whether you have difficulty seeing faces or text on TV, hearing conversations, or using a pen or pencil, Windows will provide a recommendation of the accessibility settings and programs that are likely to improve your ability to see, hear and use your computer. This has to be a good place to start.

The **Explore all settings** section below the **Get recommendations ...** link in the **Ease of Access Center** lets you explore settings options by categories. When selected, these will automatically start each time you log on to the computer. They include:

- Using the computer without a display
- Making the computer easier to see
- Using the computer without a mouse or keyboard
- Making a mouse easier to use
- Making the keyboard easier to use
- Using text or visual alternatives for sounds
- Making it easier to focus on tasks
- Making touch and tablets easier to use.

In the next few pages I will give you an overview of these various options, but I will not discuss any of them in too much detail, as different people have different and specific needs!

The Microsoft Magnifier

To start the **Magnifier**, click on **Start Magnifier** (words not icon) shown in Fig. 14.4.

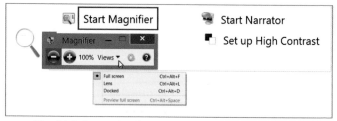

Fig. 14.4 Computer Screen with the Magnifier Active.

The new **Magnifier** window has two views: **Full screen** (the default), and **Lens**, selected from the **Views** drop-down list shown open in the composite screen dump in Fig. 14.4.

In **Lens** view, wherever you place the mouse pointer the screen is magnified.

The **Magnifier** window allows you to increase ● or decrease ● the magnification, or use the **Options** icon ⚙ to turn on colour inversion, select tracking options and fine-tune screen fonts.

If you don't use the **Magnifier** window for more than a few seconds, it turns into an actual magnifying glass icon, as shown here. Clicking this **Magnifier** icon again, re-opens the **Magnifier** window shown in Fig. 14.4.

To close down the **Magnifier**, click the **Close** button ▬×▬ in the **Magnifier** window.

This feature takes a while to get used to, but it can be well worthwhile trying it out.

Microsoft Narrator

Narrator is a basic screen reader built into Windows and may be useful for the visually impaired. It reads dialogue boxes and window controls in a number of Windows basic applications, as long as the computer being used has a sound card and speakers or headphones.

To open the **Narator**, tap or click the **Start Narrator** option in the **Ease of Access Center** (Fig. 14.2). Another way to start **Narrator** is to use the key combination ⊞+**Enter**. **Narrator** will start speaking in a rather hard to understand electronic voice reading everything that you point at with the mouse pointer.

After starting **Narrator**, an icon is placed on the **Task** bar. Clicking that icon opens the **Narrator Settings** screen in which you can:

- Change how **Narrator** starts

- Change how you interact with your PC

- Change the pitch or volume of the current voice or choose an alternative voice.

Finally, it might be worth visiting the **Narrator** keyboard commands screen to find out what commands are available to control **Narrator**. You do this by using the key combination **CapsLock+F1**. On the screen that opens, you'll find both keyboard commands and touch commands to completely control **Narrator**. While you are looking at these commands, you can stop **Narrator** from going on reading one command after another, by pressing the **Ctrl** key.

If you find this **Narrator** useful you will need to play around with it for a while until you get familiar with the way it works.

To close **Narrator** just use the key combination **CapsLock+Esc** and click **Yes** on the warning box that displays. **Narrator** even tells you that you are on the **Yes** button just before it closes down!

The On-Screen Keyboard

To activate the **On-Screen Keyboard** (Fig. 14.5), click the **Start On-Screen Keyboard** option in the **Ease of Access Center** shown earlier in Fig. 14.2.

Fig. 14.5 The On-Screen Keyboard.

This excellent virtual keyboard opens on the screen and allows users with mobility impairments to type data using a mouse pointer, a joystick, or other pointing device. The result is exactly as if you were using the actual keyboard. It has three typing modes selected when the **Options** key on the virtual keyboard is tapped or clicked, as shown in Fig. 14.6 on the next page.

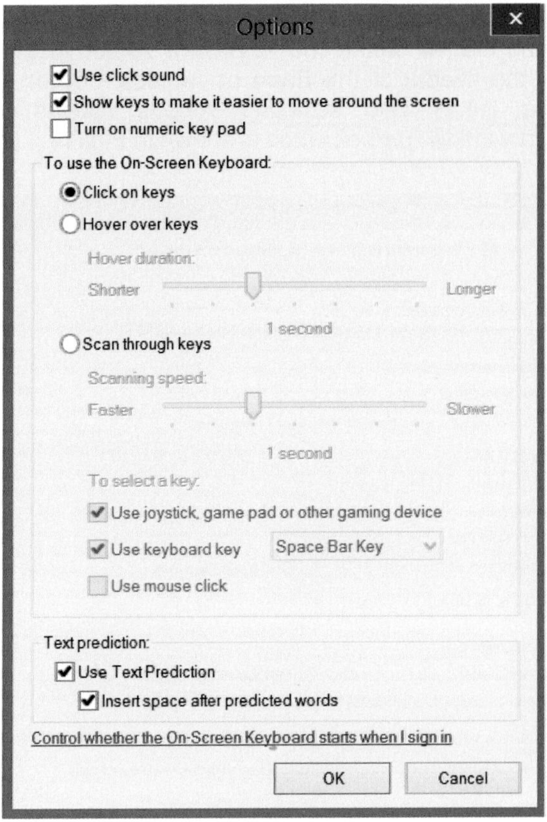

Fig. 14.6 The Virtual Keyboard Options Screen.

The three modes of the virtual keyboard are:

Click on keys mode – you tap or click the on-screen keys to type text (the default mode).

Hover over keys mode – you use a finger, a mouse or joystick to point to a key for a predefined period of time, and the selected character is typed automatically.

Scan through keys mode – the **On-Screen Keyboard** continually scans the keyboard and highlights areas where you can type keyboard characters by pressing a hot key or using a switch-input device.

You can also adjust the settings for your 'physical' keyboard by clicking the 👆 **Make the keyboard easier to use** entry towards the middle of the **Ease of Access Center** window (see Fig. 14.2), and selecting various options on the displayed window, part of which is shown in Fig. 14.7 below.

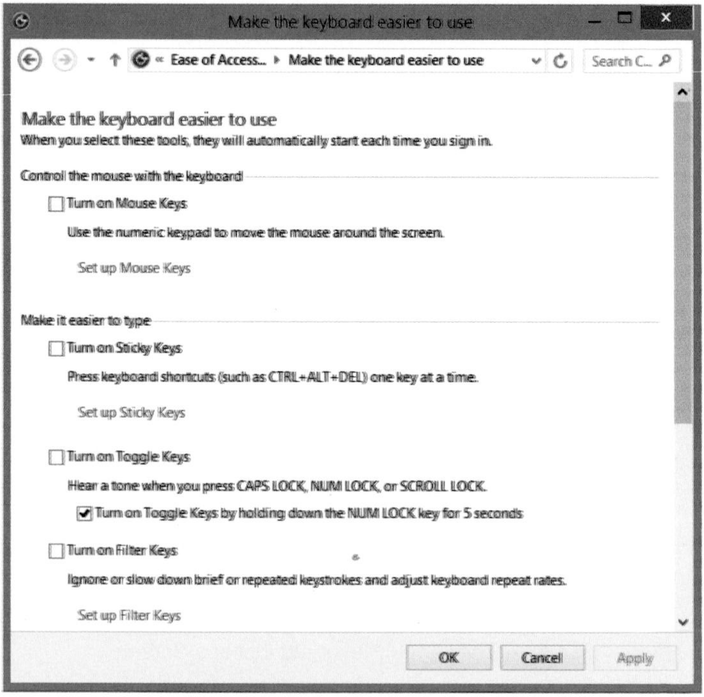

Fig. 14.7 Options to Make the Physical Keyboard Easier to Use.

On this 'Make the keyboard easier to use screen' you can:

Turn on Mouse Keys – lets you move the mouse pointer by pressing the arrow keys on the keyboard's numeric pad.

Turn on Sticky Keys – allows you to press the **Ctrl**, **Alt**, and **Shift**, keys one at a time, instead of all at the same time. This is useful for people who have difficulty pressing two or more keys at a time.

Turn on Toggle Keys – makes your computer play a high-pitched sound when the **Caps Lock**, **Scroll Lock**, or **Num Lock** keys are used. The **Turn on Filter Keys** option tells the keyboard to ignore brief or repeated keystrokes.

The Display Options

To make your screen easier to see you can try the **Set up High Contrast** option in Fig. 14.2. This opens a window, part of which is shown in Fig. 14.8 in which you can set programs to change their colour-specific schemes to a **High Contrast** scheme, change the size of text, set the thickness of the blinking cursor, etc.

Fig. 14.8 Options to Make Display Easier to Use.

The Mouse Options

Clicking the 🖝 **Make the mouse easier to use** link near the middle of Fig. 14.2, displays the window below.

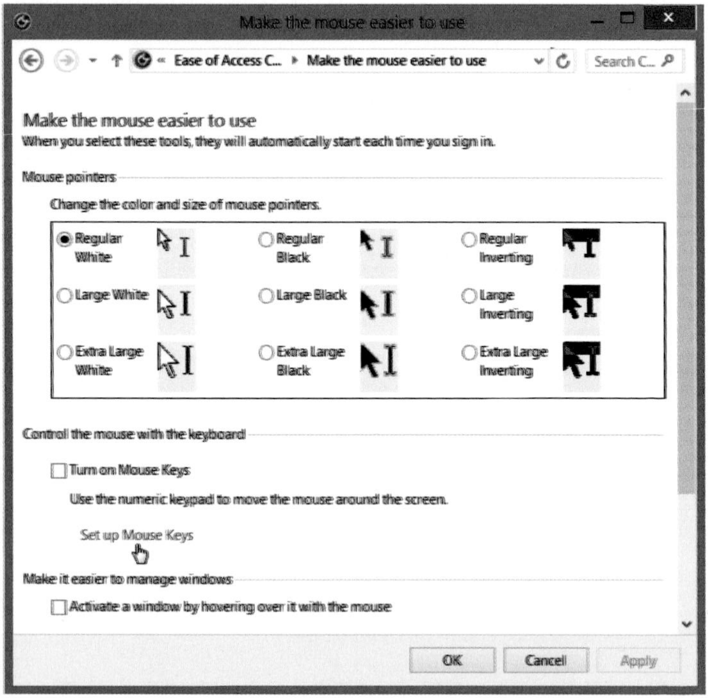

Fig. 14.9 Making the Mouse Easier to Use.

Here you can change the colour and size of the mouse pointer, and control the mouse pointer's movements with the keys on the numeric keypad.

Tapping or clicking the **Set up Mouse Keys** link, pointed to in Fig. 14.9, displays an additional window, shown in Fig. 14.10 on the next page, in which you can control, amongst other things, the speed at which the mouse pointer moves, and the shortcut key combination you need to activate and deactivate the numeric keypad.

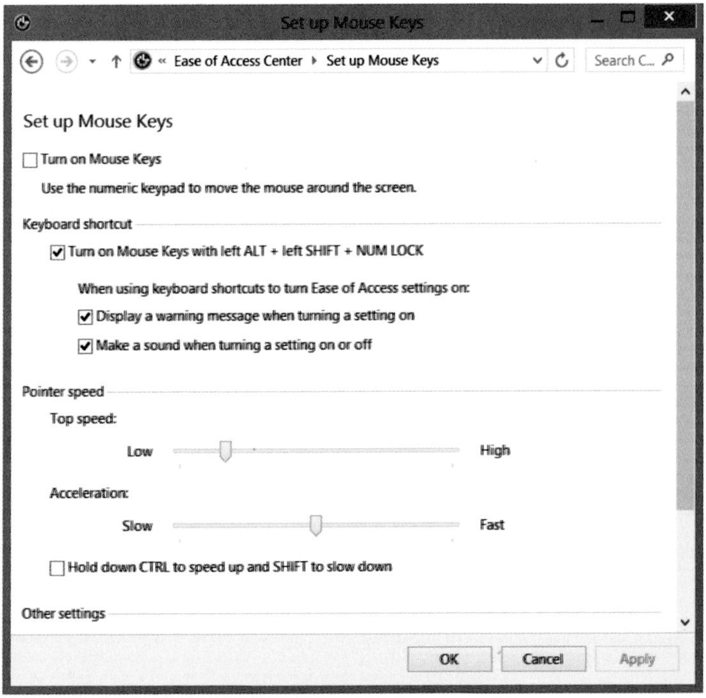

Fig. 14.10 Mouse Keys Setup.

I'll leave it to you to explore the other settings on the list in the lower half of the **Ease of Access Center**. It is the only way of finding out what suits you personally.

15

Paint & WordPad Apps

Like its predecessors Windows 8 comes with some very useful accessory programs, some of which are good enough to be ranked as 'stand alone' programs.

The Paint App

The new Windows 8 version of the **Paint** App is a genuinely useful and easy-to-use application for drawing and editing pictures or digital photographs.

By default, **Paint** is not pined on either the **Taskbar** or on the **Start** screen. So, the first thing to do is find it, using the **Search** charm, as shown in the composite screen dump in Fig. 15.1 below.

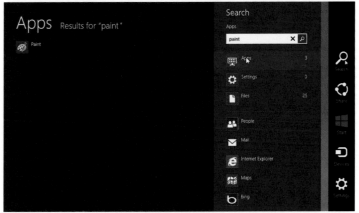

Fig. 15.1 Searching for Paint.

You could right-click the icon and pin it to the **Start** screen so that you can find it a lot easier next time you need to run it.

Starting Paint

Tapping or clicking the **Paint** icon, starts the program and displays the opening screen similar to that in Fig. 15.2 below. Here, I have used the **File**, **Open** menu command and selected a photo from the **Pictures** library.

Fig. 15.2 The Paint Screen Displaying a Photo.

You can use **Paint** to create drawings on a blank drawing area or add to existing pictures. This makes it useful for both youngsters who want to play and professionals who need a quick and lightweight image editor. With this in mind **Paint** saves its files in **.png** format by default. That is the format all the images in this book were saved in.

As can be seen, **Paint** uses the Office 2010 **Ribbon**, with the **File** button that opens the **Backstage** view, and tabs for **Home** and **View**.

Tapping or clicking the **File** button displays the screen in Fig. 15.3.

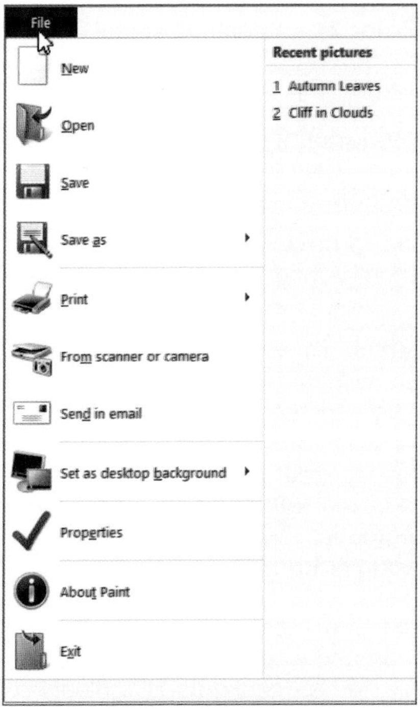

Fig. 15.3 The File Backstage View.

Many commands, that are not related to actual painting or drawing, such as **Open**, **Save**, **Print**, **Send in email**, etc., are to be found under **File**, including a list of the most **Recent pictures** you opened in **Paint.**

The **Home** tab is the one that displays all the things you use most often, such as **Image** tools to crop, re-size and rotate images, **Tools** to sketch drawings, erase them, etc., **Brushes** which includes all the brushes you might need, selection of **Shapes** and **Size** of lines and the ability to change **Color** and select from a palette.

The **View** tab has the **Zoom** tools, as well as **Rulers** and **Gridlines** for when you need to do detailed work in **Paint**.

What follows is a more detailed discussion of **Paint** and its various tools, using simple examples to illustrate some of its capabilities.

Using Paint

The drawing area (where the photo is now showing in Fig. 15.2), is where you create your drawings with the help of various **Tools**. To select a tool, simply tap of click **Tools** on the **Home** tab and tap or click the one required. Some tools can work with either of the current foreground colour (**Color 1**) or background colour (**Color 2**) – dragging the tool with the left mouse button uses the foreground colour and with the right one the background colour.

More detail of the **Tools** functions is listed below.

Tool	*Function*
Pencil	Used to draw freehand lines in either the foreground or background colour.
Fill with color	Used to fill in any closed shape or area with the current foreground or background colour.
Text	Used to add text of different fonts, sizes and attributes in the current foreground colour, with either an opaque or transparent background.
Eraser	Used to change the selected foreground colours under the eraser icon to a background colour, or automatically change every occurrence of one colour in the drawing area to another.
Pick color	Used to set the foreground or background colour to that at the pointer.
Magnifier	Used to zoom the image to different magnifications. Left-click zooms in, right-click zooms out.

With **Paint** you can draw and paint on the screen in the same manner as an artist works on paper or canvas. The tools used are actually very similar; **Brush**, **Watercolor** brush, **Oil** brush, **Calligraphy** brush, **Airbrush**, etc. However, the techniques are a little different and for the first-timer it takes a little getting used to.

Most of the tools in **Shapes** and **Size** are quite easy and straightforward to use. To select a tool, tap or click on it, and to use it move to a suitable position within the drawing area and drag the tool around to accomplish the required task. Sounds very artistic, doesn't it?

With most of the **Toolbox** options, dragging with the left mouse button uses the active foreground colour, and with the right button the active background colour. Releasing the mouse button stops the action being performed.

If you make a mistake, you can select the **Undo** button from the **Quick Access Toolbar** at the top of the **Paint**

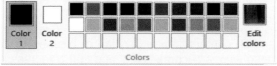 screen, also shown here, or use the **Ctrl+Z** keyboard shortcut.

The Colour Palette

At the top-right corner of the **Home** tab is the colour palette, as shown in Fig. 15.4.

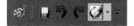

Fig. 15.4 The Colours Palette.

The two squares on the left of the above screen show the active colours which are presently in use. When you tap or click on a colour in the palette, that colour will be set as the foreground or background colour, depending on which button, **Color 1** (foreground) or **Color 2** (background) was selected at the time.

How you can use these colours with other tools, will be discussed shortly.

The colour palette shows the conventional colours that are most used in Windows. You can very easily customise the palette though, by tapping or clicking on any **Edit colors**, option which opens the screen shown in Fig. 15.5 below.

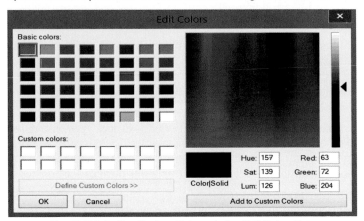

Fig. 15.5 Selecting Custom Colours in the Edit Colors Screen.

To add colours to the colour palette, tap or click on the colour selection area to place the colour picker on a colour of your choice, then move the slider to select the depth of the chosen colour.

As you move the cursor over the matrix panel, the numerical boxes below it display the colour value in terms of **Hue**, **Saturation** and **Luminosity** (H, S and L in many graphics programs), and in terms of **Red**, **Green** and **Blue** (R, G and B) content. When you tap or click the colour you want, these values become 'fixed' and that colour is placed in the **Color|Solid** box. Tapping or clicking the **Add to Custom Colors** button will add the colour to the **Custom colors** pane. They can then be selected for use in the main colour palette.

If you know the **RGB** or **HSL** value of the colour you want to use, you can enter their values into the individual boxes. Tapping or clicking the **OK** button closes the **Edit colors** dialogue box and places the customised colour on the third row of the palette.

Adding Text to an Image

Adding text to a drawing is easy. Simply choose the foreground colour for the text, then select the **Text** tool from **Tools**. The insertion pointer at that point takes the foreground colour you chose.

Next, move the insertion pointer to the working area and tap or click to open the text box by dragging it to the correct size, type the text, and in the displayed **Text Tools**, shown in Fig. 15.6, select **Opaque** or **Transparent**, the required **Font** and its **Size**, and start typing within the text box that you created.

Fig. 15.6 Adding Text to a Picture or Drawing.

When you are happy with the text, click outside the text box to paste it in the drawing and close the toolbar. However, it is possible to move a text box before pasting by hovering the cursor exactly over the dashed selection line until it changes to a four-headed pointer, as shown above, then drag the text box to a new position.

Paint and the Internet

Even with the Internet, **Paint** can be a useful tool. I show here the two main ways you can use it. One involves sending your picture or drawing to a distant friend, and the other getting pictures from your favourite Web sites.

Sending an Image with E-mail

To send the current image in **Paint** as an e-mail attachment, just use the **File, Send in email** backstage command. This opens your default e-mail program ready for you to enter the receiver's address and your message. It couldn't be easier, but don't forget to make sure the file is not too large, otherwise you may tie up your recipient's connection for too long. In fact some e-mail hosts don't allow very large files to be sent as attachments.

Copying an Image from a Web Page

Often while browsing your favourite Web sites you might find a picture that is just right for something you have in mind. No problem, apart from copyright of course, so be on your guard. I don't have such an issue here, as the picture to be used as an example is my daughter's artwork!

To copy a picture, right-click the image and select **Copy** from the drop-down menu. This places the image on the Windows **Clipboard**. You could, of course, have chosen the **Save Target As** option and saved the picture file on your hard disc, but if you want to put it straight into **Paint**, so that it can be changed (I would not dare) before it is saved, use the **Copy** command.

Without doing any more editing operations, go to the open **Paint** window and use the **Clipboard**, **Paste** option in the **Home** tab, or the **Ctrl+V** keyboard shortcut. Both of these commands paste the clipboard contents into **Paint**, as show in Fig. 15.7 on the next page.

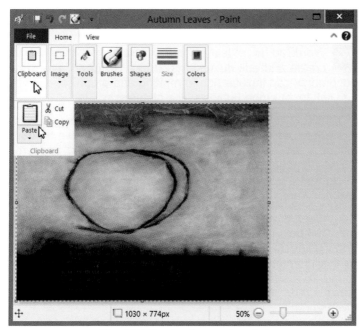

Fig. 15.7 Pasting Images into Paint.

Note that when an image is pasted, any previous selections are closed and a new selection marquee is placed around the new pasting, so that you can move it round the canvas as you like.

> **Note:** Don't forget that someone has the copyright for the image you might have selected to practice. If you want to use it in any way, you must get the permission of the original owner.

All in all the capabilities available in **Paint** result in an impressive App/program which makes it worthwhile giving it a try.

The WordPad App

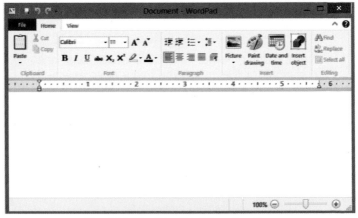 WordPad is a text-editing program you can use to create and edit documents. Unlike **Notepad**, **WordPad** documents can include rich formatting and graphics, and you can link to, or embed objects, like pictures.

The new Windows 8 version of the **WordPad** App is an extremely useful and easy-to-use application. It can be used to open and save text documents (.txt), rich text files (.rtf), **Word** documents (.docx), and **OpenDocument Text** (.odt) documents. Documents in other formats are opened as plain text documents.

By default, just as **Paint**, **WordPad** is not pined on either the **Taskbar** or the **Start** screen. So, the first thing to do is find it using the **Search** charm, as discussed at the beginning of this chapter, but you search for **wordpad** instead. Once found, it is advisable to right-click the icon and pin it to the **Start** screen so that you can find it a lot easier next time you need to run it.

Starting WordPad

Tapping or clicking the **WordPad** icon, starts the program and displays the opening screen similar to that in Fig. 15.8.

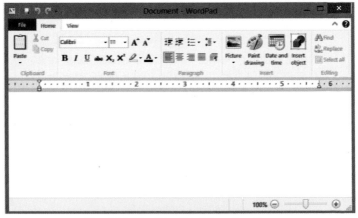

Fig. 15.8 The WordPad Opening Screen.

As with all programs that have a **Ribbon** across the top, (**Paint** for example) tapping or clicking the **File** button (or using the **Alt+F** keyboard shortcut) opens the **Backstage** menu where you can do the usual non-word processing type operations like **Open**, **Save**, **Print** and **Send in email** the current document.

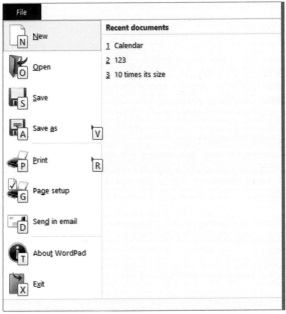

Fig. 15.9 The Backstage Menu for WordPad.

Once WordPad is open you just get on with typing your document into the working area. All the formatting and layout controls are on the **Home** tab of the **Ribbon**. To insert a picture click the **Picture** button and select its file. The **Paint** drawing option opens the **Paint** App for you to create a drawing. The **Zoom**, **Ruler** and **Status bar** controls are in the **View** tab.

Have a look at the **Quick Access** toolbar on the left of the window **Title** bar. It has icons for saving and undoing and redoing actions. You can also add more quick actions here.

To illustrate some of **WordPad**'s capabilities, you need to have a short text at hand. Perhaps you might like to type the memo below into a new document. At this stage, don't worry if the length of the lines below differ from those on your display.

MEMO TO PC USERS

Data Processing Computers
The microcomputers in the Data Processing room are a mixture of IBM compatible PCs with Intel Core Duo processors running at various speeds. Alll are fitted with combo CD/DVD drives. The PCs are connected to various printers, including a couple of colour printers, via a network; the Laser printers giving best output.

Structuring of Hard Disc
The computer you are using will have at least a 800 GB capacity hard disc on which a number of software programs have been installed. To make life easier, the hard disc is partitioned so that data can be kept separate from programs. The disc partition that holds the data for the various applications running on the computer is highly structured, with each program having its own folder in which its own data can be held.

Fig. 15.10 A Document to Type in WordPad.

As you type in text, any time you want to force a new line, or paragraph, just press the **Enter** key. While typing within a paragraph, **WordPad** sorts out line lengths automatically (known as 'word wrap'), without you having to press any keys to move to a new line.

It is assumed here that you are able to move around the text by positioning the cursor where you want it to be by using the mouse and the normal direction keyboard keys, and that you can edit the text by using either the **Delete** or **BkSp** (Backspace) keys. With the **Delete** key, position the cursor on the first letter you want to remove and press **Delete**, while with the **BkSp** key, position the cursor immediately to the right of the character to be deleted and press **BkSp**. These are rather basic skills!

If, while you are typing, you make a mistake, you can always
 select the **Undo**  button from the
Quick Access Toolbar at the top of
the **WordPad** screen, also shown
here, or use the **Ctrl+Z** keyboard shortcut.

Saving a Document to a File

When you have finished typing the text, you can save it using
the **Save** button on the **Quick Access Toolbar**, or using
the **File, Save** command on the **Backstage** screen. If this is
the first time you are attempting to save this document, a
Save as dialogue box appears on the screen with the cursor
in the **File name** field box waiting for you to type a name.
Save your document in **.rtf** (rich text format) giving it the
name **Memo to PC Users**.

If you want to save a copy of the document with another
name, use the **File**, **Save as** command which displays the
screen shown in Fig. 15.11.

Fig. 15.11 The Save As Dialogue Box.

Document Editing

Text editing is usually carried out in the insert mode. Any characters typed will be inserted at the cursor location and the following text will be pushed to the right, and down. Pressing the **Insert** key will change to **Overstrike** mode, which causes entered text to overwrite any existing text at the cursor.

When larger scale editing is needed, use the **Cut**, **Copy** and **Paste** buttons on the **Home** tab of the **Ribbon**; the text to be altered must be 'selected' before these operations can be carried out. Selected text is highlighted on the screen. This can be carried out in several ways:

a. Using the keyboard; position the cursor on the first character to be selected, hold down the **Shift** key while using the direction keys to highlight the required text, then release the **Shift** key.

b. With the mouse; click the left mouse button at the beginning of the block and drag the cursor across the block so that the desired text is highlighted, then release the mouse button. To select a word, double-click in the word, to select a larger block, place the cursor at the beginning of the block, and with the **Shift** key depressed, move the mouse pointer to the end of the desired block, and click the left mouse button.

c. Using the 'selection area' and a mouse; place the mouse pointer in the left margin area of the **WordPad** window where it changes to a right slanting arrow, and click the left mouse button once to select the current line, twice to select the current paragraph, or three times to select the whole document.

Once text has been selected it can be copied to another location in your present document, to another **WordPad** document, or to another Windows application using the **Copy** button on the **Home** tab or the **Ctrl+C** keyboard shortcut. Next, navigate to where you want the copied text inserted and use the **Paste** button or **Ctrl+V** keyboard shortcut.

Selected text can also be moved, in which case it is deleted in its original location by using the **Cut** ✂ button or the **Ctrl+X** keyboard shortcut, then moving to the required new location and using the **Paste** ☐ button or **Ctrl+V** keyboard shortcut.

Finding and Changing Text

WordPad allows you to search for specified text, or character combinations. In the **Find** mode it will highlight each occurrence in turn so that you can carry out some action on it. In the **Replace** mode you specify what replacement is to be carried out.

For example, in a long memo you may decide to replace every occurrence of the word 'program' with the word 'programme'. To do this, first go to the beginning of the document, as searches operate in a forward direction, then choose the **Replace** ᵃᵇ button on the **Home** tab to open the dialogue box shown in Fig. 15.12.

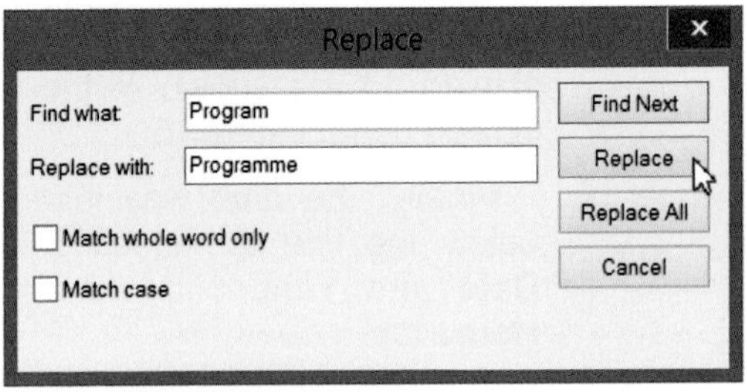

Fig. 15.12 The Replace Dialogue Box.

You then type what you want to search for in the **Find what** box. You can then specify whether you want to **Match whole word only**, and whether to **Match case**, (upper or lower case) by check-marking the appropriate boxes. Next, type the replacement word in the **Replace with** box and make a selection from one of the four buttons provided. Selecting **Replace** requires you to manually confirm each replacement, whilst selecting **Replace All** will replace all occurrences of the word automatically.

Formatting a WordPad Document

Text formatting can involve the appearance of individual characters or words, and the indentation, addition of bullet leaders and the alignment of paragraphs. These functions are carried out in **WordPad** from the **Home** tab of the **Ribbon**.

As an example of some of the formatting options, use the **Memo to PC Users** document created earlier in rich text format (**.rtf**), then highlight the title line, and change its point size to 20, then embolden it and centre justified it by using appropriate format buttons on the **Home** tab. You can also change its colour to red to make it stand out. Next, select each sub-title in turn and change their point size to 18, then embolden them and change their colour to blue.

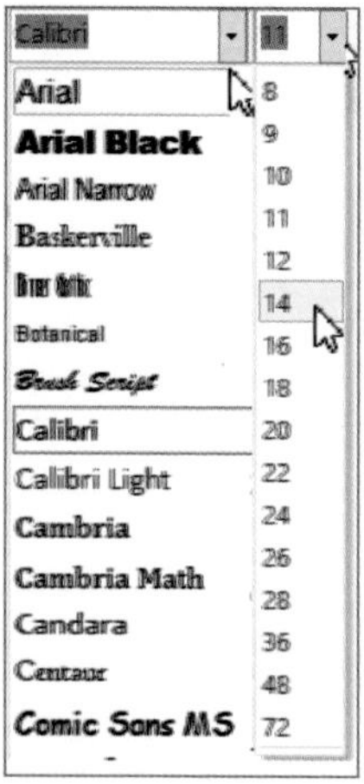

Each paragraph of the rest of the document was selected and its font changed from **Calibri** to **Arial** by choosing the font type from the drop-down list and changing its point size to 14, as shown in the composite screen dump in Fig. 15.13.

Finally, the date was inserted a line below the title by selecting the **Date and Time** button on the **Home** tab.

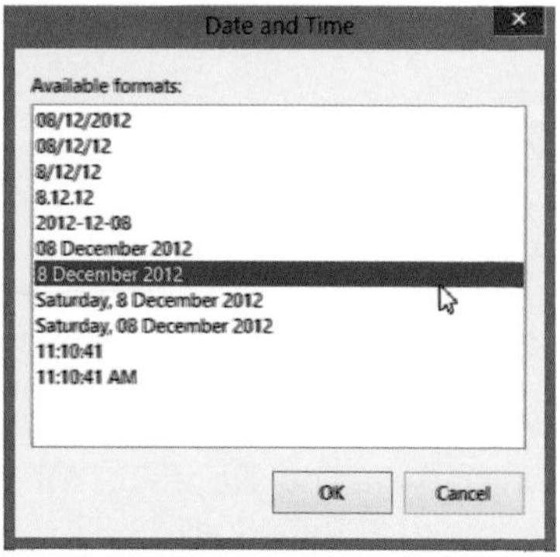

Fig. 15.13 The Font and Point Size Lists.

You can then choose a date format from the list shown in Fig. 15.14, say the one highlighted here, and right justifying it on the page.

Fig. 15.14 Date and Time Formats.

The result of all the formatting so far is shown in Fig. 15.15.

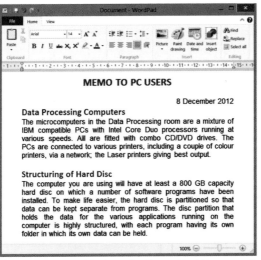

Fig. 15.15 The Display of a Formatted Document.

Formatting Lists

It is easy to create a bullet list in **WordPad**. Just type the list
as a series of separate lines, highlight them all and
 tap or click the **Bullet** button on the **Ribbon** also
shown here. This places bullets in front of each list
item as shown in Fig. 15.16

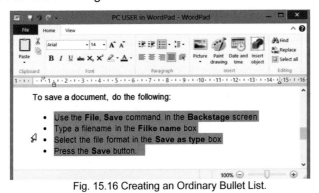

Fig. 15.16 Creating an Ordinary Bullet List.

In fact if you click the down-arrow to the right of the **Bullet** button, you'll see a list of six types of bullet 'styles' that you can choose from, as shown in Fig. 15.17.

•	1.	a.	A.	i.	I.
•	2.	b.	B.	ii.	II.
•	3.	c.	C.	iii.	III.
•	4.	d.	D.	iv.	IV.

Fig. 15.17 Types of List Styles Available.

The Ruler

The ruler is activated by default, but can be deactivated by clicking the **Ruler** box to remove the tick mark in the **View** tab on the **Ribbon**. The **Ruler** displays at the top of the text area of the **WordPad** window, and lets you set and see **Tab** points for your text, or visually change the left and right margins of your document.

Setting your own tabs is easy by clicking within the ruler where you want to set the tab. Tabs can be moved within the ruler by dragging them to a new position, or removed by simply dragging them off the ruler. Default tab settings do not show on the ruler, but custom tabs do.

Printing Documents

As long as your printer has been properly installed, you should have no problems printing your **WordPad** document. However, before committing to printing, make sure that **WordPad** is set to the same page size as the paper you plan to use by clicking the **File** button and selecting the **Page setup** option on the **Backstage** screen which opens the dialogue box shown in Fig. 15.18 on the next page. From here you can control the paper **Size** and **Source**, the **Orientation** of the printout and the size of all the **Margins** around the edge of the paper, and whether to **Print Page Numbers**.

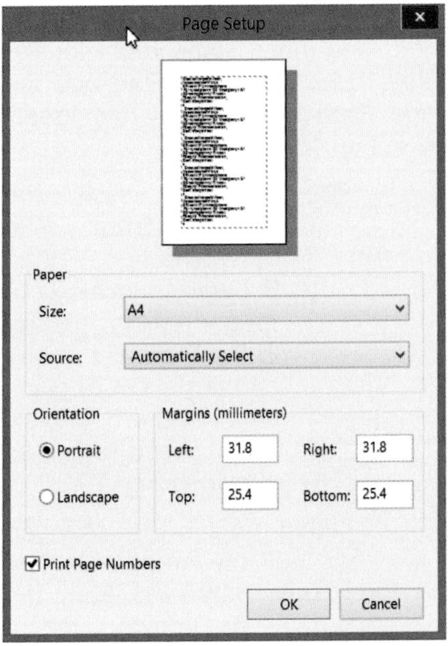

Fig. 15.18 The Page Setup Screen.

When you are happy with the printer setup, tap or click **OK** and select the **Print** button. From the displayed **Print** dialogue box you can select between different printers, including network printers (if any), and set their properties.

You can also select to preview your document before committing to paper which can save both your paper and printer toner or cartridge bills.

Embedding a Graphic into WordPad

Embedding a graphic into **WordPad** is similar to copying, but with the important advantage that you can actually edit an embedded object from within **WordPad**.

To embed a **Paint** image, first create it in **Paint**, as shown in Fig. 15.19, either in **Paint** itself or by tapping or clicking the **Paint drawing** button on **WordPad**'s **Ribbon**, shown here Paint drawing This opens **Paint** for you to create the drawing and save it as a **.png** file.

Fig. 15.19 Creating a Graphic.

Next, start **WordPad**, open the memo, place the cursor where you want to embed it, and make some room for the graphic using the **Enter** key. Now from **WordPad** use the **Insert object** button on the **Ribbon** to display the **Insert Object** dialogue box shown in Fig. 15.20.

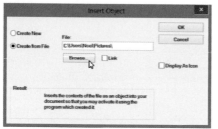

Fig. 15.20 The Insert Object Box.

Tap or click the **Create from File** radio button, then **Browse** to locate your .**png** drawing, usually in the **Pictures** library and press **OK** to place the selected graphic into **WordPad**, as shown in Fig. 15.21.

The size and shape of the embedded graphic was changed to fit where it is shown. You can edit the graphic by first right-clicking it and using the **Copy** command from the drop-down menu, then tapping or clicking the **Paint drawing** button on **WordPad** to open **Paint**. Next, use the **Cliboard** button to **Paste** the graphic into **Paint**. After you edit it, use the **File**, **Update document** option to update the graphic within the document.

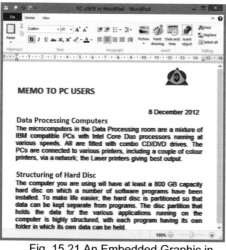

Fig. 15.21 An Embedded Graphic in WordPad.

Finally, you might need to resize and reposition the graphic to complete your work.

That is it! I hope you will continue to explore Window 8's capabilities which are far too many to include in this book.

Appendix A

Controlling Windows 8

Windows 8 functions are at their best when you learn to use the charms and finger gestures so that you can quickly jump between the **Desktop** screen and the **Start** screen, or your own programs and the new Windows Apps.

Below you will find a list of the most useful Windows 8 touch controls and their mouse and keyboard equivalents, together with appropriate screens illustrating various methods.

Displaying the Charms Bar

- Touch Control – Swipe with your thumb to the left from the right edge of the screen.

Fig. A.1 How to Hold a Touch Screen.

- Mouse Control – Move mouse pointer to the top-right or bottom-right corner of the screen.

- Keyboard Control – Press simultaneously the two keys ⊞+C (where ⊞ is the Windows key on your keyboard).

Opening the Options Menu of Running Apps

- Touch Control – Either swipe with a finger from the bottom edge of the screen upwards or, if you are holding the screen as shown in Fig. A.1, use your thumb instead.

- Mouse Control – Right-click in an empty space of an App.

- Keyboard Control – Press simultaneously the two keys **+Z** (where ** is the Windows key on your keyboard).

-

Fig. A.2 The Options Menu of a Running App.

Switching Between Running Apps

- Touch Control – Swipe with a finger, or thumb, from the left edge of the screen towards the right.

- Mouse Control – Move the mouse pointer to the bottom-left corner of the screen, then when the **Start** screen thumbnail displays, click and drag upwards.

- Keyboard Control – Press simultaneously the two keys **+Tab** (** is the Windows keyboard key).

Fig. A.3 Switching Between Running Apps.

Closing Running Apps

- Touch Control – Drag a finger from the top edge of the screen towards the bottom edge until the App minimises and disappears.

- Mouse Control – Move the mouse pointer to the top edge of the screen and when it changes to an open hand, then click and drag towards the bottom edge of the screen until the App minimises and disappears.

- Keyboard Control – Press simultaneously the two keys **Alt+F4**.

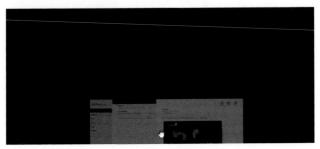

Fig. A.4 Closing a Running App.

Displaying two Apps on Screen

- Touch Control – Tap and drag an App with a finger from its top edge to the right of left edge of the screen until a thin vertical bar appears. The App snaps into place making room for a second App to display at the same time.

- Mouse Control – Click and drag the top of an App with the mouse pointer to the left or right edge of the screen. Alternatively, right-click on the App and select from the now displayed options, 'snap left' or 'snap right'.

- Keyboard Control – Press simultaneously the two keys ⊞+. (where . is the period key) to snap an App to the left or press the three keys ⊞+Shift+. to snap an App to the right.

Fig. A.5 Displaying two Running Apps on the Screen.

Zooming In or Out

- Touch Control – Place two fingers on the screen and push them apart to zoom in; pinch two fingers together to zoom out.

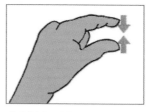

Fig. A.6 Using Fingers to Zoom Out.

- Mouse Control – Hold the **Ctrl** key down and use the scroll wheel on the mouse to zoom in and out.

Rearranging Tiles

- Touch Control – To move an App tile or a program icon to a different position on the screen, tap and hold it, then move it to a new position on the screen.

- Mouse Control – To move an App tile or a program icon to a different position on the screen, click with the left mouse button and while holding the button down, drag the object to another position.

Fig. A.7 Rearranging Position of App Tiles on the Start Screen.

Appendix B

Turning off your Computer

There are alternative methods of turning off your computer apart from using the **Settings** charm, then selecting the **Power** button.

The quickest method is to use the **Alt+F4** key combination, but for this to work you must be displaying the **Desktop**. Then, each time you use this key combination, it first closes each open App, if there are Apps opened, then and only then, it displays the screen in Fig. B.1.

Fig. B.1 The Shut Down Screen.

Clicking the down-arrow pointed to in Fig. B.1, opens a list of options to choose from, as shown in Fig. B.2 below.

Fig. B.2 The Shut Down Options List.

An alternative way is to use the key combination ⊞+i where ⊞ is the Windows key on your keyboard. This jumps to the **Charms**, **Settings**, and gets you to the **Power** button immediately, as shown in Fig. B.3. From there you can tap or click the button and select the option you need

Fig. B.3 Shortcut to Power Button.

Yet another method is to create shortcuts and place them on the **Taskbar**. Clicking such a shortcut performs the operation required such as shutting down or restarting.

The Shutdown Shortcut

To create a shortcut do the following:

• When Windows displays the **Desktop** screen, right-click it and select the **New** entry from the first displayed menu, then the **Shortcut** option from the second displayed list, as shown in Fig. B.4.

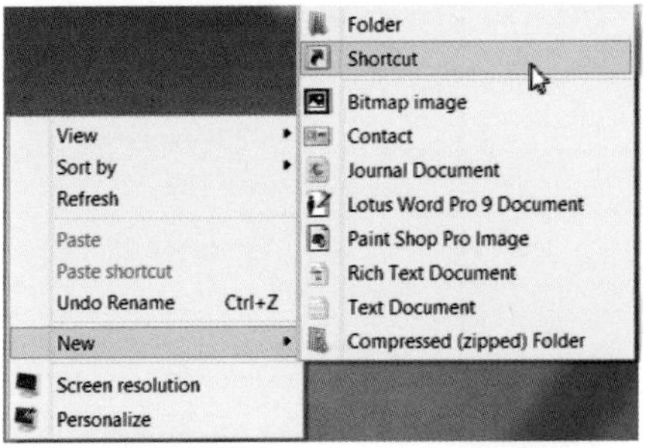

Fig. B.4 Creating a New Shortcut.

• A shortcut is placed on the **Desktop** and a dialogue box opens next to it, as shown in Fig. B.5. In **Location** text box type: **shutdown /s /t 0** making sure to include the spaces between parameters; **/s** stands for shutdown, **/t** is the time and **0** (zero) is the time prior to execution.

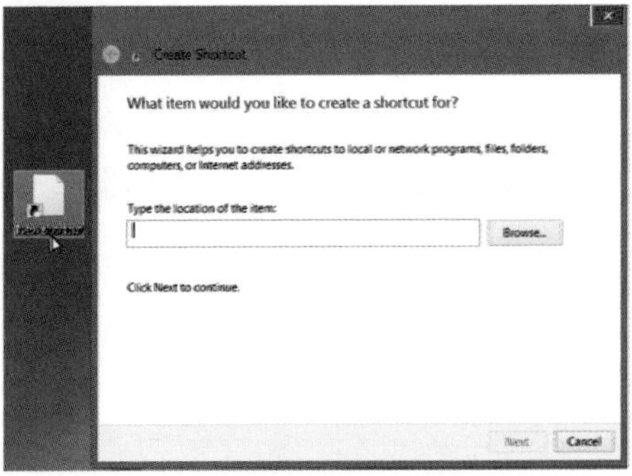

Fig. B.5 Naming a New Shortcut.

- On the next displayed screen, give the shortcut the name **Shutdown**, then click **Finish** to create it.

- Now, right-click the newly created shortcut and select **Properties** from the drop-down menu. This opens the screen in Fig. B.6.

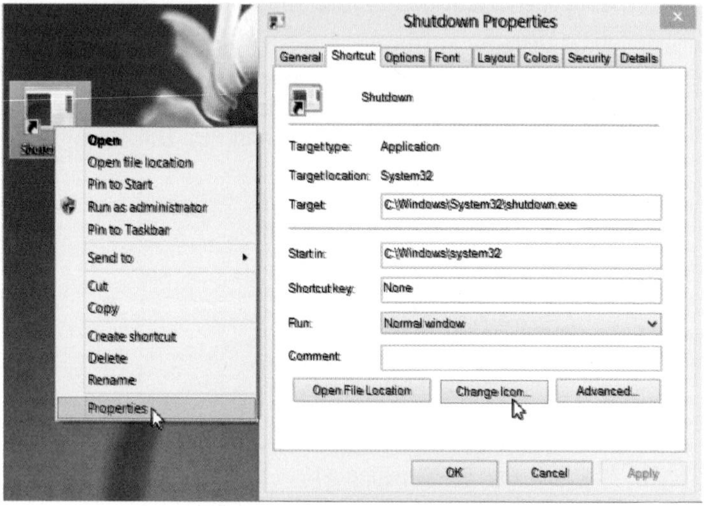

Fig. B.6 Shortcut Properties Screen.

- Clicking the **Change Icon** button in Fig. B.6, displays an array of icons to choose from, as shown in Fig. B.7. Perhaps the one pointed to might be appropriate.

Fig. B.7 Selecting an Icon to Depict the New Shortcut.

- Finally, right-click the new icon and select **Pin to Taskbar**, then repeat the right-click, but this time select **Pin to Start**. This provides both an icon on the **Taskbar** and a tile on the **Start** screen.

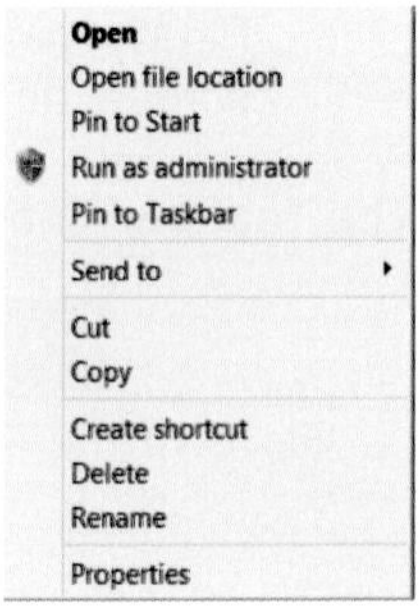

Fig. B.8 Pining the Icon to Taskbar and Start Screen.

The Restart Shortcut

To create a **Restart** button and tile, repeat the process described for the **Shutdown**, but

- Type the **Location** in Fig. B.5 as: **shutdown /r /t 0**, where **/r** now stands for **Restart**.

- The name supplied by the computer on the next screen will be **shutdown**, but you should change this to **Restart**.

- Proceed as before by right-clicking the icon, selecting **Properties** and clicking the **Change Icon** button as per Fig. B.6.

- Next select an icon to represent **Restart**, as shown in Fig. B.9. You might like to choose a different icon.

Fig. B.9 Selecting an Icon to Depict Restart.

• Finally, pin the **Restart** icon on the **Taskbar** and **Start** screen, as described for the **Shutdown** icon.

The **Taskbar** icons now look as shown in Fig. B.10 below.

Fig. B.10 The Taskbar with the Shutdown and Restart Icons.

When you finish pinning these two shortcut icons to both the **Taskbar** and the **Start** screen, then you can delete them from the **Desktop**.

Note: Please don't be put off creating these icons. It will take you much less time to do so than reading how to do it. In fact a fraction of the time it took me to write about it!

Index